"The runner does not know how or why he runs. He only knows that he must run, and in doing so he expresses himself as he can in no other way."

Roger Bannister, The Four Minute Mile

"If you want to find real diamonds, read this book! Full of wisdom, practical advice, and engaging stories, *Hiring Squirrels* is told from the unique perspective of an experienced and exceptionally accomplished professional and it is sure to help you identify individuals with true sales talent and bring out the very best in them. Peter Smith's insights can keep you several steps ahead of your competitors!"- **Patrick Sweeney, Co-Author of The *New York Times Best-Seller "Succeed on Your Own Terms"***

"Is your star hire a sales dud? Sales fail no more. Peter Smith's *Hiring Squirrels: 12 Essential Interview Questions to Uncover Great Retail Sales Talent* offers road-tested lessons to cut through the hype and magical thinking and help you interview, manage and grow the right talent for your sales team. Smith reveals who will make it and who won't, no matter how much coaching or compensation you throw their way. *Hiring Squirrels* will especially hit home with insiders in the jewelry industry, Smith's longtime stomping ground, but its step-by-step smarts are designed to fuel stellar results in all fields." — **Kim Caviness, Chief Content Officer, *McMURRY/TMG,* publisher of the jewelry authority *JCK Magazine* and *JCK online.com.***

"Peter Smith has incredible savvy and insights into the great game of sales. He is a scholar and practitioner in the field. This book is filled with his great knowledge and practical know-how. It is a great guide for anyone who wants to be more effective at building a sales team." - **Tony Rutigliano, co-author, *Discover Your Sales Strengths***

"Peter Smith is experienced, impressive and driven by a personal mission to improve professionalism in recruiting 'Winners' who bring transformational success to your business. *Hiring Squirrels* is the most practical and helpful book I have read on successful sales recruitment, providing a simple road-map to making a significant improvement to your success and helping to achieve your BHAG!" **Michael Laing, Chairman/CEO, *Laing,* Glasgow and Parkhouse, Edinburgh/ Cardiff, former Chairman of Education, *UK Jewellers Association***

"At last, a master mechanic who truly understands the inner workings of that complex machine, luxury retailing. Armed with wisdom, insight, and real world experience, Peter Smith delivers the keys to successful retailing." **Michael Han, President, _The Wedding Ring Shop_, Honolulu, Hawaii**

"In my 26 years in the luxury business, I have worked with dozens of brand managers, sales managers' business development directors, Presidents and CEOs of luxury brands, as well as hundreds of retailer owners, managers and thousands of sales professionals. No one holds a candle to Peter Smith in terms of assessing the sales and recruitment process in a retail store. _Hiring Squirrels'_ is a gift to any professional trying to come to grips with the complexities of talent management." **Haygo Demir, President, _Demir Group International, Miami, FL and Toronto, ON, Canada_**

"I have always looked forward to my meetings with Peter and to the opportunity to get his advice on having the right sales associates in the right place at the right time. _Hiring Squirrels'_ is a special and informative book that draws on his extensive knowledge of the subject of hiring sales talent." **Ezra Bekhor, CEO, _LV Luxury Holdings_**

"In, _Hiring Squirrels, 12-Essential Interview Questions To Uncover Great Retail Sales Talent,_ Peter Smith, shares his powerful insights and experience working with retail salespeople, good, bad and indifferent, in his various leadership roles. Smith's ability to break things down left me yearning already for a second book. His observations about salespeople, their behaviors and the challenges of managing disparate personalities, are told in highly relatable stories in this very engaging read. _Hiring Squirrels,_ Identifies the common pitfalls of sales teams and, more importantly, provides a clear blueprint for constructing your own successful team." **Kristin Rode, President, _KR Executive Group_**

Hiring Squirrels

12 Essential Interview Questions to Uncover Great Retail Sales Talent

Peter Smith

ISBN: 1500269271
ISBN 13: 9781500269272
Library of Congress Control Number: 2014911464
CreateSpace Independent Publishing Platform
North Charleston, South Carolina

Acknowledgements

To all the retail salespeople, managers and owners who have opened their doors, their hearts and their minds as I wandered and wondered through their lives. In particular, to my favorite sponges, Michael Han, Jim Bartlett, Cliff and Darlene Miller, Kim and Patrick Murphy, Kevin and Kathi Main and especially, to the great Gonzalez clan, Miguel and Cari. To Jennifer Carusone, Rich Pesqueira, Dave Padgett, Teri Ramirez, and Hae Yon Bagby Domingo for their great insights, their friendship and their inspiration. To Fred Levinger for the great lessons learned at Colibri. To Glenn Rothman for the world of Hearts On Fire. To Gary Hill for the kick in the pants and the always engaging chats. To Bobby Blankstein for sharing some of this journey. To Amy Bronson, without whom BC never happens, and for the two greatest gifts in my life, Ronan and Killian. To Professor Jim Murphy for your encouragement. To the late Professor John McAleer of Boston College for his inspiration. To Patrick Sweeney, without *How To Hire*...nothing happens, to Tony Rutigliano, Kristin Rode, Haygo Demir, Ezra Beckhor, Kim Caviness and Michael Laing. And, last, but not least, to Aidan and Julia for putting up with me. Thank you all for your inspiration and your contributions.

Dedication

To Sherry, for your love and support and always for the laughter!

About The Author

Peter Smith has spent thirty years building sales teams at retail and wholesale. The Irish native is a graduate of *Boston College* and of the Key Executive's Program at the *Harvard Business School*. He is also a frequent public speaker and a columnist for *National Jeweler*, where he writes about personnel, retail and branding. Smith has worked for companies such as *Tiffany & Co.* and as Executive Vice President of Brand Development for *Hearts On Fire*, where he authored the *Menu For Success*, a roadmap for retail success.

Contact information:
- dublinsmith@yahoo.com
- LinkedIn: Peter Smith
- Twitter: Peter Smith @ Hiring Squirrels
- Hiring Squirrels.com

Table of Contents

Lessons in a Blue Box

While working for Tiffany & Co. in the early 1990s, I was transferred to Houston to "fix" a store that had developed a reputation for underperformance. The store was, at that time, the lowest-volume unit in the entire chain, and the feeling within the company was that the poor results were a function of a subpar team. I had been given some credit for molding a quality team in my previous store in Chicago, as we blended newer hires with more seasoned players, and the management folks in New York felt that I could positively influence things in the Texas location.

I spent the first couple of weeks observing and quietly engaging with the employees in an attempt to understand the lay of the land. I paid particular attention to how the staff interacted with each other and with our customers and prospects. Before long, I began to draw some conclusions as to what the respective habits were for each of the specific salespeople. I paid attention to who came in on time, who was perpetually late, who took the time to positively engage their colleagues, and who did not. I watched to see who would tidy up after the had been in a showcase and who would do the bare minimum, leavi· the cleanup to someone else. I watched to see who took care of the c· tomers in a timely fashion and who was content to stand back and all others to approach customers.

At the end of the two weeks of immersion I felt like I had a pretty ſ idea of what was needed. I consulted my notes, gathered my thou and I wrote a single-page document entitled *Sales Professi*

It supposed that every skill and character trait that was not present in a given individual could be trained. I could not have been more wrong.

The reality, of course, is that the team in that store, as in most others, was made up of people who had sales wiring, people who had no sales wiring, and some folks who were somewhere in between. There were people on that team who were going to be more attentive to the housekeeping aspects of the job, and there were people who were going to leave those "distractions" in their wake, as they focused on engaging prospects and customers and on making sales.

As with all sales teams, some members of that group caused a little friction now and again and were more challenging to manage, while others gave off the impression of being model employees, as long as you didn't expect them to sell very much. Heck, there was even one guy, very experienced, very knowledgeable and with great personal integrity, who specialized in stacking Rolex boxes, or any other activity that would excuse him from having to tend to the unwelcome interruption of customers.

It took me years to realize how naive and ill-conceived that meeting, that document, and the very principle of salesperson equality really was. I could not have imagined how absolutely crazy it was to ask people without sales wiring to be great salespeople and, further, to ask people with great sales wiring to pay lots of attention to non-selling functions. It was akin to having Phil Jackson, the former Chicago Bulls coach, asking Michael Jordan and Will Perdue to swap positions to equal effect.

Great salespeople cannot be managed the same way as those folks who do not have sales wiring. Of course you can get the best salespeople to perform non-selling functions, if you manage to that outcome, but it is neither wise nor efficient to have your real sales drivers engage in non-selling functions to the same degree that the less accomplished salespeople do. When I asked Hae Yon Bigby, a great salesperson from Honolulu, Hawaii, what she liked least about sales, she answered, without hesitation, "The paperwork." To overemphasize the importance Hae Yon's responsibilities with respect to paperwork is, to a large sure, to undervalue her tremendous sales productivity.

The Common
Denominator

Over the course of my thirty-five years in business—all of which saw me either working in retail, or selling to retailers—the common denominator, and the issue that causes so much stress to managers, is that of sales personnel. I would suggest, in fact, that when I meet a manager who does not have a problem with his sales team, it is very much the exception.

To state the obvious, lousy sales teams produce lousy results, mediocre sales teams produce mediocre results and great sales teams produce great results. What may be less obvious is that many managers may not even be aware of how badly their teams are actually performing due to sales results that can either be classed as false positives (positive sales results that are less than they appear) or false negatives (negative sales results that are actually not as bad as they appear). It is very conceivable that the business might be growing with an underperforming team, or that the business might look like it is struggling, despite having a good team.

In the first instance, if you are doing a great job marketing, driving prospects into your store, if you have a great product and if you have provided a nice environment for your customers (perhaps your salespeople, despite having poor sales wiring, are very friendly and helpful) you might see your business grow. The question to be asked is what might that growth look like with a great sales team?

In the second instance, where your business is struggling, despite having a good sales team, you can take some consolation in knowing that things could be a whole lot worse were it not for the quality of the team and what you should be doing is looking very hard at the other important aspects of your business to understand why you are not seeing better results. It could be that you are not providing a relevant product anymore? Perhaps your message has changed to such a degree that you have no point of differentiation? Maybe your pricing is not relevant? It could be that your marketing has changed to such a degree that you are no longer driving customers in your door? There could be external factors, mall renovations or road repairs, etc., that are impacting performance in the short term?

One of the most challenging scenarios is if the demographics of your location have so fundamentally changed that your only long-term solution is to relocate your business. Situations like that are very hard to manage (especially if you own the building or if you are in the middle of a long-term lease) but the sooner you recognize the inevitability of your situation and begin to examine your options, the better off you will be. You do not want to get in so deep and see your customers shift their allegiance to the new mall, the new strip center, the more vibrant side of town.

Notwithstanding the aforementioned scenarios, we know that sales results directly correlate to the quality of your sales team. If you are skilled enough or lucky enough to have constructed, or inherited, a very capable sales team then you already understand the power of that single ingredient in driving your business forward. If, on the other hand, you find yourself frequently, perhaps perpetually, saddled with a weak sales team, you probably understand the damaging effects that can have on your business. I purposely say *probably understand* as it never ceases to amaze me when managers of poor-performing sales teams offer every excuse under the sun as to why the team is not performing better. They blame the stock market; they blame the banks; they blame the government; they blame their advertising partners; they blame the weather. Everything, it seems, is fair game except their own deficiencies in hiring and developing sales talent.

Even those retailers who instinctively know that they are losing business, because of their inability to build great sales teams, have little idea just how deep that problem really goes, or how much business they are losing as a consequence of this problem.

My intent in writing this book is to help you to better understand the essential characteristics of great salespeople, and to provide you with some important tools and information to help you to do a better job interviewing and hiring those candidates. Furthermore, I have chosen to focus more directly on candidates without previous sales experience, believing, as I will later discuss, that there is a vast untapped pool of potentially great sales talent in every walk of life. Despite my strong orientation towards candidates without previous sales experience, this book will also help you to do a better job of hiring candidates who do have sales experience, as long as they have the necessary wiring to be very good at sales.

The idea for this book came from a class that I taught some years ago at an industry conference in Las Vegas. The class was built upon twelve essential interview questions to ask a candidate to help understand whether he or she has sales wiring or not. To underscore the vast untapped potential of candidates without any sales experience, but who have great wiring for sales, I fashioned the questions specifically for this group.

The questions were designed to uncover whether a given candidate had the inherent wiring to be an effective salesperson in a quality retail environment. At that conference, and in the years since, I have found myself continuing to extol the importance of attracting and hiring only those people who possess the essential wiring for sales and ignoring the many candidates who, despite years of experience and despite the appearance of competence, simply do not possess the basic wiring necessary to be successful in sales.

Recognizing that there are also quality salespeople currently earning a living in sales, and that your efforts will be better served by expanding your pool of talented candidates, I have also included a separate list of questions—with some obvious repetition— that can be used to interview candidates with previous sales experience.

The questions are designed to get at the most important attributes necessary to predict success in sales. Whether you are interviewing candidates with no sales experience or candidates with sales experience, the questions will help you to strip away the rote, routine and largely ineffective standard questions that do not get at the most important characteristics and wiring.

The twelve questions are designed to understand three fundamental and very necessary traits:

1. **Does the candidate have enough *Drive* for sales**
2. **Does the candidate possess enough *Empathy* for sales**
3. **Does the candidate possess enough *Resilience* for sales**

Drive

One can debate the nuances of what labels to affix to the aforementioned attributes, but you would be hard pressed to find a superb sales professional who does not possess each of them as a central tenet in his or her arsenal. Great salespeople are driven to excel. They are competitive from the moment they wake up in the morning, and they are constantly measuring themselves against scorecards, both external and self-imposed. They are ambitious, they are optimists, they like to achieve, and they need to be recognized for their accomplishments.

Croner and Abraham write in *Never Hire A Bad Salesperson Again* that "Drive is the common denominator found in nearly all high-performing achievers in any competitive field. In fact, Drive is so important, and so powerful, that it often pushes less talented individuals beyond competitors who may have been born with higher skills but lack the burning desire to succeed."

Great salespeople seem to have endless reserves of energy and they rarely seem to switch off. In observing great salespeople in action you would be forgiven for believing that they were born to sell. For the best of them, their drive can appear to be a function of their DNA; it's as though they are born with the unique talent to sell and to persuade. Chet Holmes writes in *The Ultimate Sales Machine* that "They like control, can't stand inaction and thrive on challenges."

Empathy

The myth about great salespeople, to paraphrase Mark Twain, is that they view themselves as a hammer and everyone else as a nail and that their MO is to beat customers into submission. Have you ever heard your weaker salespeople comment about how they could never treat their customers like that? The less accomplished salespeople take a certain comfort in excusing their own lack of effectiveness by suggesting that their more successful colleagues are effective only to the extent that they browbeat their customers into submission. Nothing could be further from the truth and the living proof of that sentiment is the steady line of customers—who were apparently beaten all year long—lining up at Christmas to have their favorite salesperson tend to their needs. There are many reasons for this loyalty and one of the most important reasons is that the customer is listened to. Quite simply, the best salespeople are great listeners. They process what is being said, what is not being said and what the body language might be communicating.

George Anders writes in *The Rare Find, Spotting Exceptional Talent Before Everyone Else* that "Aggressive listeners gain authority by being incredibly attentive to other people. These experts catch the gestures, pauses, and inflections that hint at something beyond the words being said at the time." When I interviewed some of the best salespeople I know for this book, I asked them what active listening meant to them. Jennifer Carusone answered by saying, "Active listening to me means listening in an interactive way so that I can understand the person I am communicating with. This includes repeating back what I heard so that I can create an understanding and a trust between me and my client."

When I asked Dave Padgett what active listening meant to him, he replied, "Active listening for me is acknowledging in some way that I have heard the client. It might be a simple nod of my head or it could be repeating back what the client might have just said to me so he knows I am listening." Make no mistake, far from beating their customers into submission, the very best salespeople are great listeners. They seek to understand what the client's needs are and then they confidently and assuredly take charge of the situation. Teri Ramirez, another great salesperson, once told me a story of how she reached into the client's wallet and took out his credit card to process a sale that she just knew was right for him. As extreme as that might sound (and it does), it could never have happened unless Teri had done a fantastic job of building a great rapport with that client and of establishing her own credentials with him when it came to helping him to select the right gifts for his wife.

I'll leave the final word on listening to a great story teller, Peter Guber. In his book *Tell To Win*, Guber writes, "When I'm trying to either persuade someone or sell them something, the more time I spend getting them to do the talking—to tell me their story or, as it may be, their problem—the better able I am to reshape my story to address their specific challenge. The difference is being interested rather than trying to be interesting. This doesn't mean I don't prepare a story in advance. It means I stay in the moment, listening 'like a hawk,' and that what I then perceive shapes the telling of my stories. It's meant the difference between merely hitting the target and repeatedly hitting the bull's eye."

Resilience

The third major attribute of great salespeople is Resilience. In virtually every retail business we encounter, by definition, more rejection than success. If I were to take a survey of retail stores on what their conversion/capture rate is, I would guess that it would realistically fall somewhere between 20 and 40%. That means that even the best salespeople are not making a sale in potentially six out of every ten interactions. This inevitability of rejection demands a wiring that accepts, however reluctantly, that this is a reality of the job.

Great salespeople do not like rejection. In fact, they may dislike it even more than their less-accomplished colleagues. What they do not do, however, is to allow the rejection to define them or to dissuade them from the task at hand. Greenberg, Weinstein and Sweeney write in How To Hire And Develop Your Next Top Performer that "Persons with ego-strength feel as bad as anyone else would when they encounter failure, but they react to that failure much as a hungry person does to missing a meal: they are much hungrier for the next opportunity. The failure, though disappointing, does not destroy their positive view of themselves."

When I asked Jennifer Carusone what the most difficult aspect of sales is for her, she told me that understanding why a customer says "No" is her single biggest challenge. She said, "I attempt to dissect what I said and what I might have missed in my presentation so that I can learn from the experience." Apart from recognizing that there are great learning opportunities in rejection, what Jennifer was also highlighting is the manner in which great sales performers own their results. You cannot be successful in sales unless you have the psychological makeup to deal with rejection on an ongoing basis.

Philip Delves Broughton writes in The Art of the Sale, Learning from the Masters About the Business of Life, "We will see it repeatedly among great salespeople, this acceptance of rejection and failure as essential to building the muscle necessary for eventual success. They do not avoid rejection, but see it as a vaccine that strengthens their ability to resist the personal battering inevitable in a life of sales."

Rich Pesqueira told me that he doesn't believe customers when they say that they want to "think about it" and that they will come back. "I have to be careful about our mismatched sense of urgency," he said. "Sometimes the customer can pick up on the subtle clues and they might sense my frustration." About ten years ago, Rich participated in a survey that I conducted with thirty or so outstanding sales performers. About rejection, Rich wrote, "I don't abandon my approach if I fail to make a sale with a few customers in a row." Rich, like Jennifer, and all great salespeople, understands that he will not convert 100% of his interactions, but their approach and their expectation of making the sale results in a much great conversion rate than that of mere sales mortals.

Back in the early 1990s I had the unfortunate task of having to fire a man who had been a loyal and responsible employee for a store I was managing. Bill, as we will call him for this story, showed up on time every day, generally got along well with most people and behaved himself, on the whole, as you would expect of someone of his experience and maturity. Bill had many of the attributes one might look for in a retail salesperson except he couldn't sell anything. Now and again he managed to make a sale but with closer observation, we found that many of his sales had more to do with the customer having come into our store with his mind largely made up on what he wanted to buy. Bill might not have been a very good salesman but he could clerk.

After many conversations and numerous coaching sessions (most of which seemed to make Bill very uncomfortable) we finally had to relieve Bill of his duties. I remember being confounded leading up to the severance—and in the weeks and months afterwards—as to why he just never seemed to respond to the sales conversations and/or coaching. It was as though he wanted to fail and to see his employment with us come to an end.

Many years later, I had occasion to meet Bill in a different context and, I was delighted to realize, with the passage of time, any ill will over the separation seemed to have dissipated, so much so, in fact, that we agreed to meet to play a round of golf together at a future date. When the date arrived, we were greeted with the most beautiful conditions for a mid-Fall day. The weather was in the 60s, there was virtually no wind, no burning sun and we were playing on a beautifully manicured golf course with very few players. Not surprisingly, my game quickly descended to its typical level and I wondered whether I had brought enough golf balls to finish the game. The course was tough and I was playing, even by my low standards, very poorly. That said, I was caught up in the beauty of the day and, as one ball after another flew into the water, I simply dropped another ball and determined to enjoy each and every shot.

There were four of us playing together and, mercifully, no one was particularly good. That said, I began to notice Bill more and more as the game unfolded. What drew my attention to him was not so much his poor golf game; the rest of us were sufficiently engaged with our own struggles for that, but his reaction to his own game. His body language was different than everyone else's. As the rest of us laughed and guffawed at our own weak efforts, Bill seemed to be beating himself up after every shot. What's worse, he seemed to approach every shot with an expectation that he would fail and, when he delivered on his expectation, he would react like he was crushed at his lousy game. His head would bow and hang for an extended period, his shoulders would drop, or his arms would flail about in exasperation after each successive bad shot. It got so bad, that Bill would even chide himself after hitting a good shot. I could hear him admonishing himself for not hitting more of them (the good ones) or telling himself that the good shots were just pure luck, because wasn't he just awful! We attempted to distract Bill by citing the joys of the weather, the fact that we were out on a golf course mid-week, as opposed to being in our offices or on airplanes, etc.

Nothing we said seemed to break through Bill's funk and, quite frankly, his demeanor ultimately began to take away from the experience for the rest of us.

That golf game happened about ten years after I had fired Bill and it was on that course, on that day, that I finally realized why he was fired. My "light-bulb moment" was that Bill simply did not have the resilience for sales. He demonstrated in that game that he was fundamentally devoid of the necessarily resilience for any environment where rejection and/or failure needed to be managed as part of the role. Bill could not ask for the sale because he did not have the wiring to deal with the rejection that invariably came with that. It was easier for him to disengage from that essential requirement—to the point of losing his job—than it was for him to hear a customer say no seven or eight times out of every ten times he might have asked for the sale. As he appeared to be doing during the course of his golf game, he expected failure to the point that it became self-fulfilling. And, on those rare occasions when he enjoyed some success, he failed to give himself any credit at all.

Again, resilience is an essential component of sales wiring and a person who does not possess sufficient reserves of it will not be successful in sales. Or, for that matter, in golf.

Sales Wiring Cannot be Taught

I will state it now, and I will, unabashedly, return to it again and again throughout this book, that you cannot train sales wiring. You cannot build a compensation plan that creates sales wiring. You cannot dictate, cajole or insist upon sales wiring. If the candidates that you are hiring, or, for that matter, your current salespeople, do not possess the essential wiring for sales, they should not be employed in a sales capacity because they will never become very effective salespeople, no matter how much effort you put into making them so.

That is, I accept, a very uncompromising, and quite possibly dire assessment that may already have gotten under your skin. If that is so, I make no apology for the direct and possibly upsetting nature of the sentiment. I have seen too many businesses suffer too much loss as a result of hiring practices and attitudes towards salespeople that are overly optimistic and very often downright misguided. Eric Herrenkohl writes in his book *How To Hire A-Players*, "Nothing has a bigger impact on the results of your business and the quality of your life than hiring A-players." While many would intellectually agree with Herrenkohl's assessment, far too many managers continue to do the things that result in construction of mediocre or sub-par teams.

This book will help you to do a better job of identifying and interviewing candidates who possess the essential wiring to be effective in sales. With a significant emphasis on the three central elements of great salespeople—Drive, Empathy and Resilience—I have put together twelve key questions around which to build the talent portion of the interview. Recognizing that a disproportionate amount of people currently employed in a sales capacity should be doing some other line of work, I specifically focus the questions on candidates without sales experience.

You will be far better positioned to expand your pool of potential sales talent by focusing on the inherent wiring of candidates, not on their experience or unrelated accomplishments or characteristics. In fact, I will encourage you to consider and hire people who not only have no previous sales experience, but who never even knew they wanted to be in sales.

Though the primary focus of this book is on hiring candidates without previous sales experience, I have also fashioned a series of questions for sales candidates who do have some sales experience, recognizing that we do not want to eliminate that pool of potential talent. In fact, as I will discuss in a subsequent chapter, about 42% of people currently employed in sales do, in fact, have some sales wiring and are, in many cases, performing very well today.

Some of those salespeople, unfortunately for their employers, but fortunately for you, may not be performing as well as they could because they may be working in an environment that is not right for them, or for a manager who does not recognize or utilize their particular talents. Feel free to revisit the mistakes of yours truly, at the beginning of this book, as I tried to manage the Tiffany sales team as though they were all equally adept in all facets of the business.

To be clear, the focus of this book is on hiring sales talent for those retail environments where, by any reasonable standard, salespeople are expected to significantly influence a customer's decision to make a purchase. While I agree that we would all like to be treated well in whatever retail environment we elect to visit, there is a fundamental difference between going into a grocery store to load your own shopping cart than there is going in to buy a suit of clothes, buying a new car, shopping for furniture or buying an anniversary present from your local jewelry store.

Because of my own background, many of the stories in this book will involve salespeople in the retail jewelry world. That said, I will argue that salespeople who have the inherent wiring to be great will succeed in most sales environments, while those who do not have the inherent wiring will invariably struggle in any environment where they are expected to positively influence the sales process. It is very important to understand the unique aspects of your sales environment so that you can better match your needs and a given salesperson's specific talents. For instance, some salespeople enjoy a fast-paced, get-it-done-now sales process. They like the energy and the buzz and they tend to thrive when things are at their most hectic. Going into a quality retail sales environment around Christmas offers a very good example of this. You will notice that there are certain salespeople who seem to have raised their game and their energy to a whole other level. They appear to move seamlessly from customer to customer in an efficient, direct and effective style that is very impressive to watch.

Other great salespeople prefer a process that has a longer sales cycle and which has, generally, greater rewards. This might be true for great salespeople selling houses, boats, medical equipment, service programs, etc. Each of the two profiles can be tremendously effective but it is important to ensure that we put salespeople in an environment that suits their particular orientation. I know some thoroughly outstanding salespeople in the Caribbean. Their style is tremendously effective for the environment in which they work. Their sales world revolves around ships dispatching thousands of passengers for a limited amount of time on the islands on which they work. The ships' passengers descend in large numbers on the main shopping streets and move quickly from store to store, before returning to the ships and sailing away to their next destination. The best salespeople in these environments know that they must connect quickly with the passengers and exert an appropriate amount of influence to close the sale. They have to operate under the premise that there will not be a second chance to win the customer's business because they will most often be right.

The misnomer sometimes offered that these salespeople are successful because they can offer discounts to the passengers, a staple of cruise-ship environments and, as such, have a distinctive advantage over salespeople in other markets is, as far as I am concerned, complete hogwash. I say that because even in environments such as the Caribbean, and other shopping destinations where the price of many products might not be fixed, you will find the same equation between real sales performers and non-sales performers as anywhere else. The best salespeople in those environments have the necessary wiring to be persuasive and to influence and, when coupled with the requisite amounts of urgency (because that ship will sail very soon) they outsell their less accomplished colleagues by a wide margin. Those folks not blessed with sales wiring have the very same opportunity to "offer a special price" on the products they are trying to sell and yet, like their counterparts in all sales environments, they continue to underperform.

The Right Environment
for Each Salesperson

To reiterate the point I made about putting people who have sales wiring in the right environment, I will say that some of the best salespeople in environments such as I have just described would not necessarily do well in a different sales capacity. They may, for instance, become very frustrated in a role that requires a much longer sales cycle, absent the urgency and immediacy so typical in a quick-sell environment. Likewise, taking a great real estate or medical sales professional and putting her into the Caribbean to sell jewelry in the mayhem and urgency of the heavily transactional Cruise Ship business could be a mismatch. The frenetic pace and the need for urgency may not suit her at all and, despite having great sales wiring, such a hire might not work out well for the employee or the employer. Rutigliano and Brim write in *Strengths Based Selling*, "Different decision makers also have different needs and styles, and individual salespeople cannot possibly be a fit with all the buyers they encounter."

Making Bad Hiring Decisions

Most of us would probably agree that we do a pretty lousy job of interviewing sales candidates. We place too much emphasis on how someone looks or sounds, on whether they have previous sales experience or not, on the quality of their resume, and on various and sundry factors that have more to do with our own personal instincts and intuitions, and which, in the final analysis, have very little to do with the things we ought to be looking for.

George Anders writes in *The Rare Find, Spotting Exceptional Talent Before Everyone Else*, "High-profile talent mistakes generally amount to a case of heroically aiming for the wrong runway." What Anders seems to be saying is that the best and most admirable recruitment efforts are destined to fail unless there is a real understanding about what the job actually requires, before we target candidates to interview and we must then engage in a structured process to ensure those candidates have the right wiring for the roles we are looking to cast.

Two unenviable outcomes from poor recruiting efforts—and our casual, more instinctive interviewing style—is that we hire the wrong people and we don't hire the right people. One of the most-often cited laments when I meet with business owners is "I get it, I know my people are not very good but I just can't find great people." This statement is, to be frank, a fallacy. In fact, it is a fallacy that keeps on taking year after year until you break the chains of your incapacity.

There are great potential sales candidates in every single city and town and the irony is that those candidates are sometimes sitting across the desk from us being interviewed and we don't even recognize them. The reason we don't recognize and hire them is because we leave too much to chance. We trust that we are intuitive enough, smart enough and savvy enough to recognize great sales talent. We convince ourselves that our people skills and our great instincts will sniff out that super salesperson in waiting. If we were honest and objective about our own track record in hiring, we would likely conclude that we are not nearly as good as we might give ourselves credit for. If you did nothing more than list your hires for a given period—all of them—and then assign them, honestly, into one of two categories:—yes, I would absolutely make that hire again and no, I'm not certain that I would make that hire again—you would likely conclude that your track record leaves much to be desired. Most every hire felt right when you made the decision to hire them or, to paraphrase Billy Crystal's character in the wonderful film, *The Princess Bride*, "mostly" right, and yet we frequently lament having ended up with a mediocre or worse sales team.

In *Talent Flow*, Levin and Rosse write, "Everyone would like to have a selection system with perfect validity. You can think of perfect validity as a coefficient (technically, a correlation coefficient) of 1.00, meaning that everyone the system predicts will be great will be great (and vice versa). In reality, research shows that the best selection systems have validates of no great than .40–.50 and that some commonly used systems tend to have validates of about .20. This means that a substantial proportion of candidates will turn out to be poor performers." It is very hard to accept that our own great instincts, intellect and interviewing prowess could have a failure rate of up to 80%, but that is what happens when we leave the selection of talent to a process of as Anders suggested "heroically aiming for the wrong runway."

The only way to change the composition of your team is to change the composition of your interviewing and hiring processes. They simply must become more structured and less intuitive so that the best candidates are selected, and not turned away because they are not interview superstars. Likewise, the process must change so that you can more easily identify candidates who are spectacular in the interview, but who turn out to be mediocre, or worse, on the job.

So why do we swing and miss so regularly in selecting talent? For starters, we tend to hire people we like. We are drawn to candidates who look the part and who sound like they are credible for the job of selling. If something about them also reminds us of ourselves, or of they remind us of someone that we like, they exponentially increase their odds of being hired.

If the candidate does a good job of pandering to the interviewer, by offering well-placed compliments about the company and/or the product, then we are further inclined to look favorably on that candidate. If the candidate, no matter how well suited to the role, looks a certain way, acts a certain way, or reminds us of someone we do not like, it is very likely that she will never be given a fair chance to win the job.

In *Never Hire A Bad Salesperson Again*, Croner and Abraham write, "Another classic interviewing mistake is hiring someone who is just like you." We all have a natural preference for people who seem to share our values and opinions. Although this bias is helpful for making new friends, it can be a terrible thing for hiring. When you recognize that a candidate somehow reminds you of yourself, you often are blinded to the person's negative traits.

In many respects, the interview process serves as a sort of confirmatory bias, either positive or negative. If I immediately think the candidate is great, then I will see and hear that which will support my bias. If I have a negative inclination towards the candidate, for whatever reason, I will seek to support my bias by hearing and seeing only negative things from the candidate, subverting, or ignoring altogether, most of the positive attributes and stories that would otherwise emerge from the interview. In either case, if I look only to support my bias, I will be 100% correct in my assessment of the candidate. I will have rewarded (at potentially great cost to my business) my positive inclination, or I will have missed a potentially strong candidate, because I saw and heard, consciously or otherwise, only those things which underscored my immediate negative bias.

Alexander Todorov and Janine Willis of Princeton University wrote in their seminal study, *First Impressions, Making Up Your Mind After 100 M's Exposure to a Face*, "People can make judgments about a person's trustworthiness, competence, aggressiveness and likeability within the first tenth of a second of meeting them." Think about that for a moment. What they are basically saying is that in less time than it takes to read this sentence, we have already made a judgment about the candidate. What ensues, thereafter, is a journey, sometimes short, sometimes longer, that results in the interviewer carrying that immediate judgment, that positive or negative bias, through the interview process and, all too often, making a hire or no-hire decision on the basis of an uninformed judgment that took less than one-tenth of one second to form. What we actually deliver is the illusion of a fair and balanced interview.

There are, of course, lots of interviews where you will not consciously or unconsciously form an immediate impression upon first meeting the candidate. What follows, while absent the effects of confirmatory bias, is rarely much better inasmuch as it focuses too much time and effort on the things that don't matter, and too little time on the things that do matter.

Sex is another reason that we make very bad hiring decisions. As Malcolm Gladwell wrote in the *New Yorker*, "For most of us, the job interview functions as a desexualized version of a date. We are looking for someone with whom we have a certain chemistry, even if the coupling that results ends in tears and the pursuer and the pursued turn out to have nothing in common. We want the unlimited promise of a love affair."

In the luxury retail world, we are selling products that are often very stylish, high-priced and sexy, and we harbor a notion that the employee, man or woman, ought to exude sex appeal. The reality of the "sex hire" is that we are successful in getting what we want. We hired someone who looks the part and who, unfortunately, may be all wrong for the business of sales. This scenario has been called the *Halo Effect*, and dozens of studies have shown that we automatically ascribe better qualities and higher attributes to good-looking people than we do to those who were not so fortunate in the gene pool lottery. If it is any consolation, know that far more important hires have been made, far higher up the executive and political ladder, as a consequence of the *Halo Effect*. The ranks of CEOs and top executives are filled with folks who were perceived as a better fit than others, when what often made the difference was not their intellect or wiring, but the fact that they "looked the part," a consequence of being a little taller and better looking than their shorter colleagues.

The *Halo Effect* in luxury retail does not fill the ranks with taller people, but it most certainly does ensure that there is entirely too much emphasis on the way someone looks, as opposed how they are wired. I can't begin to tell you how many times I have walked into luxury retail environments to find attractive people throughout the store who are stylishly dressed, finely coifed and woefully inept in the role of sales professionals.

The aforementioned hires might be mistakenly referred to as safe hires. They look the part, they dress the part and they are often very pleasant people. They may even come with multiple years of experience. They are, however, all too often, one of the worst hires you can make. The absence of the most basic of sales characteristics and their inherent lack of drive ensures that they will close fewer sales, deliver a lower average ticket per transaction, and that they will, on the whole, be far less likely to engage in activities and actions that drive business and satisfy customer needs.

They will not be particularly good at cross-selling, up-selling or clientelling—and that's just one day's worth of shortcomings. Amortize those misses over a year's worth of selling days and you will conclude that your business stands to lose hundreds of thousands of dollars, or even millions of dollars, as a result of their shortcomings and the attendant and ongoing missed opportunities. At a minimum, it should have you redefine the idea of what a "safe hire" is.

Welcome Assertiveness

Another reason we miss making the right hire is that the very wiring of great sales producers can be quite off-putting. This can be equally true for candidates without sales experience, who possess sales wiring, as well as candidates with sales experience. They tend to be more assertive and more confident in their abilities and this can come across as a little too cocky for many interviewers. These candidates have the ability to take the interview by the scruff of the neck, and a casual observer might be forgiven for wondering who the interviewer and who the interviewee is.

Unlike weaker sales candidates, who can very often come across as very agreeable, very pleasant, wholly unlikely to make the interviewer uncomfortable, great sales wiring will shake the apple tree in demonstrating the very characteristics that make them great closers. They don't passively wait for the customer to point to a piece of jewelry when they are engaged on a sales floor and they understand that it is their responsibility to help that customer make the very best choice—and now. That sense of urgency, that expectation and drive is not trained into great salespeople. It is inherent and, as such, it has to be expected, and welcomed, in the interview process.

Chet Holmes, in *The Ultimate Sales Machine*, writes, "If you don't understand the personality profile that makes top performers salespeople, you might just turn them away after interviewing them. A high-influence candidate can seem overly eager in a job interview—maybe even come on too strong. Don't let a little bravado put you off; it is the essential ingredient in every superstar."

Great salespeople are not generally model citizens. When it comes to crossing their *t's* or dotting their *i's*, they can leave a trail of baggage in their wake and they are oftentimes difficult to manage. These traits and shortcomings will generally emerge throughout the course of a thorough interview and, unfortunately, a decision to hire or not to hire is often made on the strength of these perceived foibles or shortcomings.

I have a friend who has been a consultant to retail business owners for many years. She is very accomplished and she has great passion and love for retail. In the course of her work, she often spends time with sales teams and she seems, on the surface, to have a great understanding of the dynamics of retail sales personnel. Despite her wonderful pedigree and her many years of experience, I recently learned that she was building a profile of great salespeople to deliver to her clients and in that profile, she inserted language that spoke to how the sales candidates fit into the team, executed great follow-up, adhered to the rules, etc. In short, she was insisting that successful candidates ought to be great "team players."

To say that I was surprised by this would be an understatement in the extreme. Great salespeople are not followers of rules. They are not always detail-oriented, and they can be at times connected and yet separate from the team. The best of them accept their responsibilities in a team environment, and they want to be liked and accepted. However, when push comes to shove, they will frequently eschew the wants of the team in order to drive sales results. Goffee and Jones write in the *Harvard Business Review*, "Great retail businesses depend on characters who do things a bit differently. Over the years we have had lots of them. We must cherish them and make sure our systems don't squeeze them out."

The behavior of the most successful salespeople sometimes costs them style points with their colleagues and makes them difficult to manage. This drive, and its byproducts, are the very reason that they are so successful. They refuse to lose sight of the goal, the prospect, the sale—and their competitive drive ensures that they will, more often than their less accomplished colleagues, put themselves in front of customers. Their wiring does not readily fit into a neat box and any efforts to apply layers of must-haves, which do not align with their competitive drive, is a recipe for failure. This single-minded assertiveness can be threatening to lesser performers, who would prefer to have everyone get along and to not put too much pressure on prospects and customers. If you do not have the capacity or the will to accommodate highly driven and higher-maintenance characters you will struggle to find and retain great sales performers. Mark De Rond writes in *There Is An I In Team*, "High performers' ambition and intensity occasionally mean they can be explosive in how they deal with those around them."

There is a tradeoff in hiring good performers; you will have to manage some amount of baggage but the returns for doing so can be very, very healthy for your business.

Toxic is Out

Any manager who is serious about developing a high-performance team must understand the inevitability of hiring some offbeat characters. That said, by no means do I advocate hiring or retaining salespeople, regardless of their wiring, who are highly disruptive, overly self-absorbed and morale-killers. If the behaviors of the driven salesperson create a hostile work environment, and undermine the efforts of the team, they need to be gone. There is a big difference between accommodating the eccentricities and peccadilloes of a sales driver and tolerating bullying, disruptive or hostile behavior.

While there should be some acknowledgment of the inherent tensions that can exist between high performers and poor performers, there should always be an expectation of respect, civility and common courtesy for customers, vendor-partners and colleagues. This does not mean that tensions cannot and will not occasionally blow up and cause dissension and conflict that will require the attention of a good manager, but behavior that is unapologetically hostile and disruptive should not be acceptable in any business.

Occasional blowups can be the result of the high performer exhibiting frustration at perceived obstacles being placed in her way, but it also holds that disrespectful and dismissive behaviors by her colleagues, with water cooler gossip and alienating words or actions is equally disruptive and very costly. As John Maxwell writes in *Winning With People*, "A person with a negative self-image will expect the worst, damage relationships, and find others who are similarly negative." Weaker salespeople can fall into a trap where they view their more accomplished colleagues as 'the bad guy.' This often results in finding like-minded people and engaging, sometimes consciously and sometimes unconsciously, in a campaign to discredit the successful sales driver.

A jeweler friend of mine in Houston once took his top sales producer outside of his store and pointed to the name on the building. He told the salesman that he had lost sight of who owned the business and that it was time for the salesman to go work someplace else. It was a very courageous decision by my friend and he naturally worried about the repercussions of terminating what was at that time a $2 million sales writer. As it transpired, the positive effects of his bold decision were felt immediately and his business went on to bigger and better things. There is a fine line between accepting some challenging behaviors and personalities and tolerating individuals who undermine your efforts and poison your culture. I would like my top producers to understand and embrace their responsibilities as team players, even as I know that when push comes to shove, they will default to a more assertive approach and occasionally rub some people the wrong way.

Know What You Are Looking For

By better understanding what you are looking for, by embracing the immense value that candidates without sales experience can bring to your business, and by adhering to a defined and more structured approach to interviewing, you can profoundly impact the composition of your sales team and exponentially improve your store's sales performance.

If there was ever any doubting the need for great sales professionals, with the ability and the will to engage customers, to close sales and to make things happen, the internet should serve as a reminder that you had better start placing a much higher premium on getting business done every time a prospect enters your store. That commitment to closing sales with urgency is not in lieu of providing customers with a great experience—if we fail to do that, why do they need salespeople or brick and mortar stores at all? It does mean, however, that we need to take a hard look at the criteria that we use to construct our sales teams.

The notion of having a lot of *nice people who get along*, while failing to capitalize on the multitude of opportunities presented in your stores each and every day is a certain recipe for failure, perhaps even catastrophe. It is my hope that this book will help you to shape a sales team and a culture that addresses the needs of today's customer and business climate.

Hire Squirrels and Stop Training Horses

I n his funny and poignant little book, *You Can't Send a Duck to Eagle School*, Mac Anderson asks the following question: "If I told you that your company mission was to climb a tree, would you train a horse or hire a squirrel?" Anderson captures perfectly the reality of what so many luxury retailers have been doing for years—namely, hiring and training horses to climb trees. In the course of reading this book you will come to understand the extent to which the vicious cycle of poor hiring has killed many brick and mortar businesses and is threatening to damage many more. More importantly, I hope that you will find in these pages a different approach to your current hiring process and that you will recognize that a few simple changes in thought and approach can fundamentally transform your talent management and, consequently, positively drive your business forward.

Why Luxury Retail?

I have specifically identified luxury retailing as my target audience, not because the approach outlined in this book won't work in non-luxury retail, but because the professional salespeople that I reference generally have the capability to make considerably more compensation than might generally be available in a mass-market or in a heavily price-oriented environment, where clerking and/or service is often prized and needed more than sales acumen. I will define luxury retail as any store where salespeople are expected to positively influence the customer's choices and where there exists a clear opportunity to develop a strong relationship ongoing. Some obvious choices would include jewelry stores, clothing stores, shoe stores and, of course, better quality department stores.

Essentially, luxury retail is any brick and mortar store that sells what some might call luxury or discretionary products. I'm not a huge fan of the term "discretionary" personally as I think it fails to give proper credence to the tremendous emotional benefits that can often come with luxury purchases, whether they are self-purchase or gifts. Silverstein and Fiske write in Trading Up, "The emotional space is the most personal and immediate and, for many American consumers, the most important. It is about goods I buy now to make me feel as good as I can, as immediately as possible."

Contrary what weaker salespeople think, customers do not go into stores to kick tires. Believing that customers will not buy is the single best recipe to ensure that you will be correct. There is a self-efficacy about negative thinking that, if it could be turned into lotto numbers, would make millionaires of huge numbers of really bad salespeople. Pablo Picasso once said, "He can who thinks he can, and he can't who thinks he can't. This is an inexorable, indisputable law." I'm assuming that Pablo was a little too busy in his world to bother with trivialities such as drive, resilience and empathy as prerequisites for the fellow that "thinks he can" but I agree with his general principle. If you believe the customer is not going to buy, you'll be right often enough to be a lousy salesperson.

What's in Your Pocket?

In a visit with a retail client in New Mexico a couple of years back, I had occasion to chat with the sales team during a quiet period when there were no customers in the store. In the course of the conversation, one of the salespeople offered, in discussing a particular jewelry brand, that "Not everyone can afford to buy that," a look of smug satisfaction on his face, as though he had just delivered some profound utterance for the eternal betterment of his assembled colleagues.

I responded by asking the salesman if he would be kind enough to turn his pockets out and, after a brief and quizzical couple of moments, in which he and everyone else wondered what I was up to, I requested a pair of scissors from the store manager. After a deliberate, and quite welcome, moment of expectant silence from my friend and his colleagues, I informed the group that I was now going to cut the pockets from his trousers so that he would immediately and forevermore cease and desist the practice of spending from his own pocket.

The nervous chuckle from the salesman confirmed that the point had been received and, I suspect, he was delighted to retain the full and unhindered use of his trousers, pockets and all.

Humor aside, I went on to explain that it is not our job to decide what the customer should spend, any more than it is up to us to decide what value they should place on any given item. It is our job to fully engage each customer as a unique individual, with the aim of understanding what their particular motivations and needs are and attempting, through open-ended questions, and active listening, to fulfill their needs, not to project ours. I told them that it is not our job to rescue them from what we believe to be high prices, or from products that might be beyond the scope of what we think they can afford.

Despite the fact that the store sold $30k–$50k watches, the salesperson had already concluded that people were not going to spend the required amount of money to purchase the diamond brand in question. I was disappointed that I did not have a sketch artist traveling with me so that I could have had him build a composite of what the customers who would buy that brand might look like. It is a rare talent to know so precisely what someone is and is not capable of spending, and I have no doubt that we all could have benefited from a sketch to make all of our jobs that much easier.

It is infuriating to encounter salespeople who think they know what a customer will or will not buy. It would seem to be much more enlightened, and infinitely more rewarding, to believe that every single customer has the means and the desire to buy the products and brands that their store offers and to invest their energy in finding out what the customer's needs are. You will not sell to everyone, but you will make many more sales and positively engage and satisfy many more customers. As Broughton writes in *The Art of the Sale*, "Optimism and pessimism turn out to have a compounding effect on success in sales." Who knew?

Hire the Wiring

For more than thirty years, I have worked with, hired, trained, fired, celebrated and championed good, bad and indifferent salespeople. I have had the benefit of working with hundreds of salespeople directly, and with thousands of salespeople indirectly, in my various roles on both the retail side of the equation and on the wholesale side. I have had hundreds of conversations with owners and managers of retail stores about their personnel challenges and the need for improvement in this critically important area. Without question, the challenge of shaping the sales team seems to be the common denominator across all of the businesses that I have dealt with. Not surprisingly, another resonant theme is that the vast majority of business owners readily admit to being woefully inept at identifying, interviewing and hiring great salespeople.

I had the good fortune of working closely with *Caliper* from Princeton, New Jersey for more than a decade. My company used the *Caliper* assessment to determine the characteristics and wiring of potential new hires. We also used the assessment to measure the wiring, collectively and individually, of entire sales teams already in place at retail stores. This later use of the *Caliper* we called the *Personnel Landscape*, and it was a very effective way of looking at the composition of a team based on the individual wiring of each salesperson.

As effective as it was to understand whether a given individual had the requisite wiring to be successful in sales, it was even more so, to see how the team mapped in the collective. I have seen managers of businesses shed tears when reviewing how their teams measured up when looking at wiring on the *Personnel Landscape*. The good news, even in the worst of those situations, is that it can be repaired one employee at a time. Just one great hire can make a major difference and serve as a catalyst to ignite profound change.

Let's go back to Mac Anderson for a moment. What he is suggesting in his question about horses and squirrels is that you are either a salesperson or you are not. You either have the necessary wiring for the job or you do not. Of course, the many training companies that ply their trade by convincing you that you can, in fact, teach a horse to climb a tree would take great umbrage with Anderson. Their very existence demands that you have a blind faith in their capacity to make pigs fly. Okay, I exaggerate.

Trainers and training programs are only as effective as the raw material (talent) they have to work with. It is probably unrealistic to believe that people who make their living by training will tell you that they will simply not be successful with many of your salespeople, but that is the statistical probability. Have you ever wondered why your sales team seems to emerge from training sessions all fired up about what they have learned only to resort, within days, to their old behaviors and level of performance? Buckingham and Clifton write in *Now,*

Discover Your Strengths, "If you learn a skill, it will help you get a little better but it will not cover for a lack of talent." Why do you think that is?

Did you pick the wrong trainer, the wrong training? Or is it, to paraphrase Mac Anderson, that horses will never learn to climb trees no matter how much you train them?

More than 50% of Salespeople are in the Wrong Job

B y any reasonable standard, more than half the people employed in sales do not have the wiring for the job and no amount of training will change that. You can, of course, teach product knowledge; you can give them directions on language and approach with customers. You can offer them pointers on how to greet customers, how to overcome objections, how to capture information for your CRM initiatives. All of those things are very relevant and very helpful. They are great for those people who already have sales wiring but they are, at best, short-term fuel for people without sales wiring. These folks will often take the best notes, respond as though they have just been given a magic potion, and perhaps even show an immediate improvement. What you will not get is a sustained game-changer for the majority of salespeople. There is something quite admirable and empowering in believing that we can train a horse to shimmy up a tree but the underlying truth in most retail training approaches is that a well-trained horse is better than no horse at all.

I agree completely with Anderson's sentiment. My experience has shown is that one either has the wiring to be a great salesperson or one does not. There may be little consolation in that sad reality if you find yourself with a team that is mediocre, or worse, but the good news is that there are large numbers of people out there who do, in fact, have the wiring for sales and many of them don't even know it yet. You just need to rethink your process for identifying and hiring them. Again, the good news is that a single great hire can be a very important first step in shaping a performance culture, and fundamentally changing the way you view your talent-building process.

Great salespeople can and do come from all walks of life. They are schoolteachers, dental hygienists, bartenders, bus drivers, college graduates, high-school dropouts, flight attendants, cheerleaders and every other group you can think of. *Caliper* makes the case that as many as 24% of the general populace have the inherent wiring to be effective salespeople. If that is true, then a process that is no more scientific than pointing to strangers on the street would provide a better success rate than what many retailers are doing today. We are clearly not suggesting that as a strategy but I make mention of it because it does give hope that even moderate refinements in your approach to talent acquisition can give you better results than what you might currently be doing.

One of the complaints I hear echoed from retail managers and owners is "I'm not a human resource person, this is not what I do." With very few exceptions, the entire process of employee management is rarely a strength of people who are, by definition, required to wear many hats in their business, from marketing, to finance, to facilities manager, to merchandiser, etc. When you add human resources to that partial list, you begin to see why so many of these managers view hiring as a necessary evil and that cycle of under-performance is destined to continue until that attitude is finally changed.

In Anders' *The Rare Find, Spotting Exceptional Talent Before Everyone Else,* he references a study by business strategist, Marc Effron, that surveyed a group of 1,800 human resources professionals at big companies. "He asked if they thought they were winning the war for talent. Only 18 percent of respondents said yes." If four of five human resource professionals at big companies believe that they are not doing a good enough job in talent acquisition, you can appreciate the challenges facing small and medium-sized retailers who do not have the luxury of dedicated HR professionals in this important area.

Change the way you Interview

The interview process is the single most important factor in your talent acquisition process. It is, quite frankly, where you make your biggest mistakes. This book will help you to redefine your interview process and greatly increase the likelihood of you making better hiring decisions to significantly improve your business results. The book features a serious of twelve questions that will help you to identify the essential wiring in sales candidates who have little to no previous selling experience and who are either coming out of school and embarking on their career, or who are currently working in a different field altogether.

Recognizing the need to look at the inherent wiring of candidates— as opposed to the myriad other factors that can often distract from the really important matters necessary for sales success—I have fashioned the questions for candidates with little to no sales experience at all. I believe that there is an exciting pool of candidates employed in all manner of jobs who would be well-suited for a sales career.

Accepting that there are also candidates with sales experience who do, in fact, possess good sales wiring, I have also added some additional questions with a focus on these more experienced candidates. Again, in looking at candidates with sales experience, I would implore you to set aside matters such as years of experience, pleasant personalities and product comprehension until you have satisfied yourself that these candidates first have the necessary wiring for sales.

Some of the questions can serve equally well for candidates with and without sales experience. For instance, *"Describe a situation where an idea of yours was rejected and tell me how you felt about that"* is a question that can work very well for both experienced and inexperienced candidates. It offers a wide-open space for candidates without experience to draw from without penalizing them for not having previously worked in sales. He or she could easily describe a school project or a social situation to answer that question. An experienced sales candidate might draw from a work-related experience, or they might select something from outside of work. In either case, it gives you an opportunity to see how willing the candidate is to tap into what might have been an unpleasant experience, how he handled the rejection, and whether or not he used that rejection as a learning experience.

Another question that can serve equally well for both experienced and inexperienced sales candidates is, *"When you are shopping, what kind of salesperson impresses you?"* The question is designed to give a person without sales experience an objective way of telling you how they view the role of a good salesperson. The question can be equally relevant for a candidate with sales experience. You might think that an experienced candidate would understand exactly what the interviewer is getting at when you ask this question, but guess what? You are just as likely to hear her talk about friendliness, product knowledge and no pressure to buy. She may not mention the importance of listening, the relevance of asking probing questions, understanding and satisfying the customer's requirements and the need to actually sell something.

As difficult as it is to see retailers make poor hiring choices, and we should all know how costly those mistakes are in a sales environment, I am particularly saddened by the amount of potentially great sales candidates who are interviewed and then passed over, because we are looking for the wrong things. We respond to people who are nice, who make us feel comfortable, who have enough experience to satiate any concerns we may have about the potentially heavy burden of orientation. We pass them over because of our own personal biases and because the more assertive candidate seemed to take charge of the interview in a way that might have made us uncomfortable. As Chet Holmes writes in *The Ultimate Sales Machine*, "People with strong ego will have no problem telling you how good they are. Contrary to conventional rules of etiquette, this is actually a positive thing in a top producer and you want to give them the opportunity."

The interviewing process, around which much of this book is focused, is made up of three parts: Culture Fit, Resume Exploration and Wiring, which is to say uncovering the essential and inherent traits necessary to be successful in a sales role. While I will briefly speak to the first two parts, I will be focusing most of the discussion on the third element: uncovering wiring. This is the area in which we struggle the most in the hiring process and it is the single biggest factor in determining whether a candidate will or will not be successful in sales.

Most competent interview professionals are pretty adept at assessing the quality of a resume. They can also generally work their way through the progression of jobs and responsibilities as indicated on the resume. Even novice interviewers can spot a few interesting and relevant accomplishments to discuss on a resume, whether that is from a recent college graduate or from someone with ten years worth of experience.

The issue of culture fit tends to be a little more challenging. That is generally the case because we either have not taken the time and effort to articulate and/or commit to writing down what the central elements of our own culture are, or because we know the elements pretty well but we believe that we can train, teach or indoctrinate any new hire into our culture. I would argue that culture fit is decidedly more complicated than that and I will expand upon that subject in a subsequent chapter.

Great Salespeople May Not Be Your Favorite Interview Subjects

It is worth repeating that great salespeople can be very difficult to manage. They don't always cross their t's or dot their i's and, metaphorically speaking, they can oftentimes leave carcasses in their wake. The traits that make them successful, hard-driving, unrelenting and unapologetically direct can drive coworkers and managers crazy. In short, great difference-makers cannot be managed the same way as mediocre and poor performers and they do not interview the same way. They may have a little edge to them; they made be a little more direct than you would like; they may even appear to be interviewing you.

If you are transitioning from a casual "we-want-everyone-to-get-along" culture to a more performance-based culture, there is every likelihood that there will be ruffled feathers as you make that transition. Great performers don't often have patience for non-performers and their stronger personalities can rub people the wrong way. You need to honestly assess whether you are fully committed to making a transition such as this as it can be a challenging process. It can also be a very lucrative game-changer for your business.

Have you ever heard mediocre or poor salespeople complaining about how a strong performer goes about his or her business? "I would never talk to my customers that way," they say. "Can you believe how he just ignored that lady and waited on that other customer?" Poor sales performers have a tendency to find each other and a strong fear of anything (new people, new sales plan, new compensation plan, etc.) that might expose their shortcomings. They also have a highly inflated sense of their own self-worth in a sales environment.

Great producers do profile prospects and they will occasionally upset customers who they deem to be not sufficiently serious to warrant their attention. They use their brilliant radar to guide them to where the fish are swimming and it is this remarkable intuition that makes them immensely effective, difficult to manage and, if you'll forgive the generalization, not always the most popular members of your staff.

There is no small irony in the aspersions cast by lesser performers against their more successful colleagues. It typically centers on the assertive manner in which the strong salespeople target prospects and yet, having converted many of them into sales, those customers come back time and again to seek out the same salespeople who were supposedly overly assertive with them in the first place.

The reason for that loyalty has a good deal to do with the fact that the customer's time is being respected when they come into the store. They appreciate the fact that the real sales producers do a better job of assuming ownership in the sales process and help lead the customers to solutions for their needs. John Kawhon writes in *Selling Retail,* "When asked how they feel about their products, salespeople who succeed reveal that they have one thing in common. They are convinced that everyone would be better off if they were enjoying the benefits of the product they're selling." Great salespeople find a way to powerfully and passionately connect the needs of the customer to the benefits of their products.

Poor sales producers, on the other hand, have a ridiculous notion that when a customer responds to their inane "How can I help you?" with "I'm just looking" that they are telling the truth. They are not "just looking." There is always a reason why prospects come into your store and they don't want to have to indulge someone who has neither the talent nor the inclination to take care of them. When I asked Rich Pesqueira, one of the best salespeople I have ever been around, what he most enjoys about the sales process, he replied that he likes to "inspire action." Regardless of why the customer says they came into the store, Rich always adopts the position that they really came in to buy something, to take care of a specific need. It is precisely because of that mindset that Rich has been so effective over the years in closing sales and satisfying customers.

All Salespeople Are Not Created Equally

While it is admirable to believe that all salespeople ought to be managed the same way, the reality is that we simply cannot adopt the same posture with great sales performers as we do with their less-accomplished colleagues. If we value stellar performers, then we simply must recognize—just as a baseball team recognizes the value of a pitching ace, a football team recognizes the value of a great quarterback, and a soccer team recognizes the value of a great goal-scorer—that great salespeople need be managed differently. The sales superstars readily shoulder the responsibility to continually produce sales at the highest level in a way that is not easily understood by their less productive colleagues. They take it upon themselves to drive results every single day and they are generally very hard on themselves when they don't produce.

Great sales talent comes with the batteries already included. They are pre-motivated, if you will. While they certainly need to know that their efforts are respected and appreciated by their managers, what they really crave is the validation that comes with producing great results, with seeing their name in lights, with checking the scorecard. Great salespeople are already motivated to achieve and, if they find themselves in an environment that gives them the freedom to express their talents and the positive affirmation that comes from being appropriately compensated and occasionally celebrated, they will start their own engines and drive hard to be successful every day.

What's Coming Out the Other End

When I speak with small business owners about what their plans are to take their businesses to the next level what I often hear are marketing solutions (we're going to run this and that event, we've started advertising on such and such radio station, we invested x amount of dollars in our digital marketing or social media initiatives, or we have redone our website). All of these things are interesting and worthwhile but may, in fact, be nothing more than self-delusional and wishful thinking, absent the essential ingredient of great sales talent. To illustrate this point in a presentation, I once put up a picture of a funnel. Into this, I dumped every conceivable expense related to running a retail business. I put marketing dollars, public-relations dollars, product dollars, facilities costs, training costs, compensation plans, financing, etc.

After metaphorically dumping all of these costs into the funnel, I showed the very small opening at its mouth and labeled that "salespeople." The point I was making, of course, is that no matter how well you think you are spending your dollars on all of the many areas that require investment, you are, to a large extent, completely at the mercy of your sales team through which all of that spending must filter. Customers can respond positively to your great marketing and public relations initiatives; they can enjoy your facilities and your products; they can even enjoy your "friendly and experienced salespeople," but if the sales team fails to execute effectively, the entire effort and expense will be diminished.

While no one doubts the need to spend appropriately on advertising and marketing initiatives, it is very difficult to measure the results. There is a reason why we continue to hear the time-worn axiom quoted over and again, "50% of my advertising is effective and 50% is not. I just don't know which is which." Here is a way to think about growing your store's business that might just be a whole lot easier than trying to figure out which 50% works and which does not. If your sales team is currently converting three of every ten prospects who visit your store and you can improve that ratio to closing four of every ten prospects, you will have grown your business by 33%.

That simple ("simple" as in easy to understand, not "simple" as in easy to do) improvement would have a profound impact on your business. So how would you do that? Is that a function of spending even more money on advertising? Is it easily achieved by expanding, upgrading or improving your store? Will it happen if you spend even more money on products by bringing in a new brand? All of the aforementioned can, and should, be a part of your thought process in considering where your business is headed, but the most basic and most obvious answer is to hire salespeople who will do a better job closing more sales—and to give them the opportunity to be great.

Great Salespeople Have Higher Batting Averages

Great salespeople close more sales. They close sales at a higher average ticket than less capable salespeople. They up-sell and cross-sell more, and they do a better job of clientelling. If you accept those facts and you spread those better results across each selling day, each week, month and year, you can begin to comprehend the massive difference in results between great salespeople and their less productive colleagues.

A Commitment to changing the way you interview and select your sales talent is the key to revolutionizing performance on your sales floor. Baseball often serves as a great metaphor for business and I offer the following example as a way to think about your sales talent.

In 1942, Ted Williams, the great Boston Red Sox hitter, batted .407 for the season. In all the years since that momentous season not one single player in Major League Baseball has come close to matching that average. In fact, no player since 1942 has batted even .400. What is remarkable about that statistic, is that Ted Williams, in that historic year, a year that has survived even the steroid era of falling records, actually *failed* more times than he succeeded. For every ten times that Ted Williams went to the plate that season he failed to get a hit six times and yet he stands as the player with the highest single-season batting average in baseball for more than seventy years.

What distinguished Ted Williams, beyond his considerable baseball talents and his remarkable eyesight, was his mindset. He expected to get a hit every single time he went to the plate and it was that self-confidence; that expectation of success; that single-minded focus on achieving his goal, which helped to propel him into the history books as perhaps the greatest ever hitter in baseball.

Great salespeople go to the plate every single time with the expectation of getting a hit. They don't allow the occasional ground-out, or the occasional strike-out to derail their plan. Ted Williams did not change his batting stance, or his approach to hitting on those occasions that he failed at the plate. He was unbelievably well-prepared, hyper-focused and imbued with an expectation of success every time he stepped into the batter's box. He was also an incredible talent.

Williams was asked by Maxwell Stiels of the *Boston Globe* why he did not sit out the final Sunday double-header in that historic season. He went into the final day batting over .400, but if he had suffered a bad day at the plate during the two scheduled games it could have cost him his place in the history books. Ted replied to the question by saying, "I figured a man's either a .400 hitter or he isn't." Williams' poignant response captures perfectly my own sense of great salespeople: they either are or they are not and, as Terry Francona and Dan Shaughnessy wrote in *Francona, The Red Sox Years,* "The science of hitting does not reward those who try harder." One cannot be a great sales producer by trying harder; they must first have the fundamental wiring. If they do, then the training and relevant experiences will propel them to their own historic seasons.

The Experience Myth

"Get rid of sad dogs who spread doom." David Ogilvy

As I write this, I am flying in an airplane somewhere between Phoenix and Boston. It is snowing quite heavily in Boston and I can tell you, without a modicum of hesitation, that I am very comforted to know that we have an experienced pilot on this plane to navigate my safe passage. I am also thinking about a wonderful experience I had last night in Scottsdale, where I got to listen to President Bill Clinton at the event I was attending. One of the questions that was asked of the president was what mantra or little saying would he offer to his daughter as she goes through life. Mr. Clinton thought for a few moments and responded, "Get caught trying." He went on to explain that he had attended all but one of his high-school reunions and that the next one he would attend would be his fiftieth. The president talked about the accomplishments of many of his classmates and, as he reflected on the slowly dwindling numbers of his high-school classmates, he said that the one common theme that seemed to haunt some of his friends was regret at not having tried, while they had the opportunity, to do what they loved.

Listening to Mr. Clinton tell the story of his reunions, and hearing him note the sadness and regret felt by some of his classmates was a very poignant moment for me. It seemed to have resonated with others in the audience too, as I saw postings on Facebook later that night, some of which referenced the quote. "Get caught trying" is great advice for everyone, but it does not work if one of my fellow passengers decides to invite himself, absent the training and inherent wiring necessary to be a great pilot, to fly the plane. It will not serve a patient on an operating table if the hospital janitor decides that day that surgery is his opportunity to "get caught trying." My landscaper will not likely deliver any sweeter music than the sound of his lawnmower if he decides to bang away at my piano keys in a valiant effort to tune my piano. The "get caught trying" applies equally to the all of the aforementioned if they want to try some new endeavor like writing a book, singing with a band, taking a carpentry course, or even if they want to take flying lessons. You can no more expect someone without the inherent wiring to be a great salesperson than you can ask the hospital janitor to perform surgery. Of course the consequences are not nearly as grave but the point should not be quickly dismissed.

If I am flying, I want a pilot who is experienced. If I am having surgery, I want a surgeon who is experienced. If I am hiking a mountain, I want a guide who is experienced. The premise of experience and competence, so often true in surgeons, pilots and mountain guides, does not hold true in sales. There is simply no validity to the notion that salespeople become more effective sales producers by being in the job for more years. Nor is there any reason to believe that giving them the benefit of numerous training programs and initiatives, or better compensation programs, makes them any more capable of performing well in a sales capacity. In fact, depending on which studies you want to believe, the statistical probability that a person currently employed in sales is actually in the wrong job is somewhere between 50 and 60%.

Show of Hands for all that Experience

Some years ago I was teaching a class to independent business owners at an industry conference in Las Vegas. The annual seminar provided training, marketing and branding sessions for up to one thousand salespeople, managers and owners of jewelry stores throughout the US, Canada, the Caribbean, the UK and Australia. During a morning session with about 150 owners, I was asked whether I felt like there was a correlation between competence (producing sales results) and experience in sales. The questioner went on to speculate that it would be reasonable to expect that someone who was around longer, who had the benefit of more training, and who knew more about the products, would necessarily be more effective in sales.

I replied by asking the owners to raise their hands if they could boast of having a least one Graduate Gemologist (GG) on their sales team. Becoming a GG requires a level of commitment from the store and from the employee and the requirements are generally met over a period of years while the employee works in the business. Still other people elect to get their GG straight out of school, and, as such, might not have a lot of actual retail jewelry sales experience.

By definition, having a GG on staff reasonably assumes that the person in question has many years of experience in the retail jewelry business and, most importantly has an impressive working knowledge of most of the variables and machinations of diamonds and color-stones. In other words, they have the training; they know as much or more about the products that they are selling than their less educated colleagues and so they ought to be the best salespeople, right?

When I asked the owners for a show of hands if they had a GG on staff, about two-thirds of the room (about 100 people) responded positively. I then asked those people who had raised their hands to leave their hand up in the air if that person, or those persons on staff who were GG's, were also sales champions, as defined by the specific brand that I was representing. To become a sales champion, one had to meet certain criteria in sales performance, placing them amongst the elite salespeople.

Statistically, there should have been about one champion for every five stores represented at the conference. When the hands started to drop, it became very clear that there was not only no correlation between training/experience and sales performance, but, in fact, there may well have been an inverse effect. There was not one hand left aloft; not one GG had also become a sales champion.

I was so intrigued by the result of this impromptu study that I decided to ask the same question to the second group of owners in the afternoon session. I prefaced the question by recalling the setup from that morning's session, without sharing the result. Once again, I asked for a show of hands from those business owners who had at least one GG on staff and, once again, I asked for the hands to be left aloft if that person was a sales champion. The result was identical from the morning session. Not one single hand remained aloft; not one single owner from either of the two sessions could claim that a GG from their staff was also a star salesperson.

Was I surprised by the result? Yes and no. I was not at all surprised that there was a very low incidence of competence in one discipline, cognitive learning, parlaying into another, sales acumen. Neither was I surprised that multiple years of sales experience did not correlate to sales proficiency. I confess, however, that I was surprised that there was not a single example of a GG also being a sales champion. The orientation towards the science of gemology (though it could have been the science of just about anything else) is an entirely different wiring than that of someone who is fundamentally wired to engage with customers, to persuade and to sell.

As I will discuss in a later segment on training, I am not criticizing all of the salespeople who chose to further their education, and their understanding of gems and gemology, by committing to the process of becoming a graduate gemologist, with the attendant GIA (Gemological Institute of America) accreditation. Having someone on the team who really understands the nuances of gems, gemology and metals is essential, particularly when it comes to buying products for the store, writing appraisals, handling special requests and repairs, etc. There are always customers who want to know every imaginable detail—in some cases to the point of absolute torture— and it is helpful to have someone on staff who can take care of the "engineer type" as necessary. Those types of customers, however, are the exception. While they strike fear in many retail salespeople and seem to have an inexhaustible appetite for technical details, they are not the norm.

Even in the age of information overload, with every fact and fiction available on our mobile devices, most customers are not looking for salespeople to tell them everything they know about product, they are looking for a solution for their needs and the best salespeople deliver that solution with the minimum amount of information necessary. The GG types, in every business, have a tendency to summon the Oscar Wilde quote: "Like all people who try to exhaust a subject, he exhausted his listeners."

I have seen too many salespeople over the years talk a customer out of a sale. They continue to product and information dump, never asking for, and never expecting, the sale, until the customer is almost worn out and has to leave. They'll sometimes even offer to give the customer even more information to take with them, in case they weren't exhausted by the information they already had.

For perspective, consider the following from David Lewis' *Impulse, Why We Do What We Do Without Knowing It*: "It has been calculated that from the dawn of modern civilization to 2003, a period of around 5000 years, human activity generated around five exabytes (that is five billion gigabytes) of information. Between 2003 and 2010 the same amount of information was generated every two days. By 2013 it was generated every ten minutes." With that kind of information assaulting our senses each and every waking moment, is it any wonder that shoppers cringe when they find themselves faced with a salesperson that doesn't understand their needs, isn't listening well, and persists in information dumping, in lieu of a real human connection.

My impromptu study in Las Vegas underscored my belief that salespeople who are drawn to, and highly engaged by every nuance and product detail are not usually wired for the art of persuasion and sales performance. In the jewelry business, for instance, they are likely to wax poetic about the four Cs (clarity, color, carat weight and cut). They might even jump into crown angles, light-dispersion and refractive indexes. Beyond their embrace of the science of products, some of these types of salespeople can also be very pleasant and very patient with customers. Those are very good qualities and there could be a place in many stores for those types.

What they do not do very well, however, is to close sales and influence customer behavior. Of course, there are exceptions. While my informal polling of 300 people at the industry conference did not uncover a single example of a GG also being a superstar salesperson, I do, in fact, know of a few. My point is that they are very much the exception. They tend to lack the competitive drive that very often defines great sales performers and hiring managers put too much stock in skills, experience and industry education, even as none of that determines whether someone will be a good salesperson.

If your business is selling luxury, couture clothing, fine jewelry, cars, vacation packages, fine wines, your salespeople must have the requisite product proficiency to be effective. It would not reflect well on your products, your people, or your business to have false information given out to your clients and prospects. Your customers would not reward your business with their trust if they were getting misleading product information or little to no information at all. Can you imagine walking into an Apple store or a Tiffany store and having salespeople who did not know what they were selling? That said, while you can teach product information to someone who is wired to sell, you cannot teach the motivation to sell to someone who does not have it. Despite his years of experience, that horse will never learn to climb a tree no matter how many climbing lessons you give him.

We're All in Sales

Many years ago I worked at a company called Colibri, in Rhode Island. I served as director of marketing for the one of their divisions and, consistent with the culture of the organization, that meant that my role started at the very beginning of the product development process and continued, directly and indirectly, through the sales process. One of the great challenges that my division had encountered over the years was the seemingly impossible task of penetrating one of the giant office supply chains with our products.

No matter what items we introduced to market we could not penetrate the big and potentially exciting juggernaut. Enter yours truly. I made it my personal goal to tackle the account myself and to attempt to do what our salespeople had not been able to do: get an order and develop a business relationship. Over a period of months, I was able to develop some exciting new products that I thought would work very well for the big chain and, after a very productive and exciting meeting at their corporate office, I secured what was for our company and division a very sizable opening order.

When I returned to the office later that day, the CEO of Colibri, Fred Levinger, asked me how the visit went. I replied, maintaining the kind of decorum that suggested I had been in the end-zone a time or two in my career, that I had managed to secure an opening order of about $250,000. Levinger, without missing a beat, responded as only he could, by telling me directly and somewhat crudely, "That isn't shit, come back to me when it sells through."

Whatever excitement I had felt about making the sale soon vanished and I left feeling very agitated about the bucket of cold water that the CEO had just poured over my head. The sale had been the byproduct of a huge amount of work on my part over a period of months and I had proven that we could penetrate the big retailer.

After Levinger's comments, I returned to my office and spent a few minutes licking my wounds. I reasoned, as someone who did not work directly in sales, and who stood to make no commission or bonus for my efforts, that my win had been terribly underappreciated and I felt like the CEO's response had been harsh and completely de-motivating.

Within about five minutes, I started quietly laughing to myself. It suddenly dawned on me that I had just received one of the best business lessons I would ever receive in my career. Notwithstanding Levinger's directness, he had taught me two hugely valuable lessons:

> ➤ **That we are all in sales, regardless of our title or perceived role.**

> ➤ **That sell-through is the ultimate barometer of a successful sales relationship.**

In the most literal sense of the word, selling through (which would make the office-supply buyer successful) or selling to a retail customer (so that they can look like a hero and/or feel great about that purchase after the fact) is really the only barometer that counts.

My four years working for Levinger was a journey that I will never forget. It was fraught with challenges and frustrations and, in many respects, it could sometimes be a lesson in how not to treat people, as little premium was placed on professional and civil discourse. That said, the lessons about sales and salespeople still resonate to this day, many years after having worked there and several years after that company was sadly mismanaged into oblivion by a future ownership group.

Levinger often cited the mantra that we are all "two-legged overhead" and he would regularly extol the necessity of getting out in front of our clients by telling his people that they were costing him money when they were in the office. I hadn't realized, before working for Colibri, the extent to which we are all salespeople—and the responsibility that we all have for moving the ball forward, directly or indirectly. There were certainly many places I had worked prior to that experience, and since that experience, where there existed some kind of invisible, but nonetheless visceral line of demarcation between those people in sales and those people not in sales. What Levinger instilled in me, and in anyone else who had the good sense to look beneath his sometimes rough exterior, was that we are either advancing the sales process or we are wasting time and money. Our specific jobs may have been in product development, marketing, credit, customer service, manufacturing or human resources, but he expected everyone to share in a single vision of driving business forward in whatever manner they could.

The product development people needed to engage the sales team and the customers to understand what needs were not being met, what opportunities existed that would excite our clients and their customers. The marketing people needed to come up with programs independently, and in cooperation with our clients, that would help to drive awareness and traffic to their retail stores. The credit department needed to ensure a speedy resolution on all matters related to smoothing the way for our clients to get product quickly to their customers and to ensure credit procedures that were healthy for our company and for our clients. The customer service team needed to deliver answers and solutions with good grace and expedience that enabled our clients to get satisfactory resolution for their customers. Manufacturing had to produce orders of a quality that met or exceeded our clients' expectations and in a timely fashion to ensure that out-of-stock situations were kept to a minimum. And Human Resources had a huge responsibility to ensure that the very best candidates were hired for each available job—and that there were always suitable candidates in the pipeline to avoid unnecessary gaps in any position that might negatively impact our customers.

Fred Levinger created a culture of accountability at Colibri such that every single employee quickly learned he or she was an essential cog in the wheel that kept the sales engine running. Those employees who learned that lesson enjoyed more successful careers than those that did not understand that basic premise - regardless of what their specific role was in the organization.

Team Dynamics and the Personnel Landscape

O ver a five year period I conducted a survey of 700 salespeople, from more than 100 retail jewelry stores, using the *Caliper* Assessment. *Caliper* is a company based in Princeton, New Jersey, that has produced a very effective assessment to determine the inherent characteristics and wiring of a given person, and the likelihood of that individual being a good fit for a given job. The *Caliper* test measures a range of traits across four specific categories:

- ➤ **Persuasiveness**
- ➤ **Interpersonal**
- ➤ **Problem Solving/Decision Making**
- ➤ **Personal Time/Time Management**

The company then measures the areas of strengths and weaknesses and determines whether the candidate will be a good fit for the job. For my purposes, we were using the *Caliper* to determine fit for sales positions in retail jewelry stores. While we often looked at the *Caliper* results for pre-employment purposes, we also used the assessment to look at the composition of existing sales teams. This enabled the store owner to understand where her strengths and weaknesses were across the whole staff. As revealing as a single *Caliper* might have been, looking at the composite results for the whole team was very enlightening. We called the combined results the *Personnel Landscape*.

The *Personnel Landscape* consisted of four distinct columns into which each of the salespeople was assigned based on their Caliper results. The four categories were identified as:

> **Hunters**
> **Farmers**
> **Hybrids**
> **Wrong Business**

After each salesperson took the *Caliper* assessment, the results would determine whether he or she was best categorized as a *Hunter*, a *Farmer*, a *Hybrid* or a *Wrong Business*. The *Hunter* represented a hard-driving, very transaction-oriented salesperson. The *Farmers* also had good sales characteristics but they tended to be a little less driven and have a more patient selling style. The *Hybrids* were those rare people who possessed the best characteristics of the *Hunter* and of the *Farmer*. And lastly, *Wrong Business* were those people who, regardless of their tenure or other fine characteristics, were clearly not wired for sales. This was the largest of the four categories by far, with 58% of all salespeople falling into the "not-really-salespeople" column.

Having tested more than seven hundred salespeople, we found that 25% of the employees were classified *as Farmers*, 13% were classified as *Hunters* and only 4% were classified as *Hybrids*. As mentioned, the largest single category was *Wrong Business*, with 58% of people classified into that category.

A person who is classified as *Wrong Business*, regardless of his experience, regardless of his education, is considered to be ill-suited to a role in professional sales. He can possess some very admirable characteristics, such as a strong service orientation and a good team player. He may be very people-oriented, and he may generally be a loyal and dedicated employee. Despite those, and other very positive traits, he simply does not have the drive, the ambition, or the wiring to significantly influence a customer's behavior. Furthermore, if asked to describe what they do for a living, many *Wrong Business* employees will hesitate to refer to themselves as "salespeople," preferring, instead, to describe themselves any other way. This happens because they can have a misguided sense of the role of a salesperson. They would prefer to believe that their job is to be nice to customers, to have good product knowledge, to demonstrate a good work ethic. All of those attributes are positive and should be valued. They do not, however, compensate for the absence of drive, empathy and resilience—all absolute imperatives in the makeup of effective sales producers.

Once again, I will acknowledge that the aforementioned attributes are very positive and, ideally, you would see them in your best sales producers. However, an overreliance on those attributes, instead of the real difference-makers, accounts for almost six of ten people being identified as *Wrong Business*, rather than the more desirable, *Hybrid*, *Hunter* or *Farmer* categories.

With such a large percentage of salespeople in the *Wrong Business* category, you can imagine how disturbing it was for many retail store owners to view their own *Personnel Landscape*. While it would sometimes take a few minutes for the harsh reality of his predicament to sink in, the prospect of what might be possible by redefining his hiring practices would ultimately energize the owner. By showing him how many *Hybrids*, *Hunters*, *Farmers* and *Wrong Business* people he had on his team, he was able to determine his needs in a more targeted way than if it were to simply uncover a need for more good salespeople.

For instance, *The Personnel Landscape* may have indicated that his team had plenty of *Farmers* but not enough *Hunters*. A scenario such as that could result in lost sales, as the *Farmer* style, despite having good sales wiring, tends to have less urgency to close sales. If his *Personnel Landscape* were to show that he had too many *Hunters*, it might explain why his team occasionally experienced more friction and in-fighting than might be comfortable for the business. In the main, however, it was generally less about the mix of *Hunters* and *Farmers* (*Hybrids* were statistically much more difficult to find) than it was the abundance of people in the *Wrong Business* category.

Again, someone who does not have the fundamental wiring to be a salesperson is going to cost you business every single day, in every interaction. Even when they do make sales, they will very often resort to a lowest common denominator, with any sale seeming to suffice. To compound matters, credit is often directed their way for a job well done when, in fact, the sale may have been a fraction what it otherwise could have been in the hands of a competent salesperson. The latter will typically account for a larger average ticket, a consequence of up-selling, cross-selling, etc.

It is important to understand that the 58% in the *Wrong Business* column are only identified as such to the extent that they are being measured against people with sales wiring. They are not *Wrong Business* if the business owner or hiring manager places a greater premium on customer service skills and likeability than on driving sales. I have worked with far more business owners than you can imagine who say they want to hire great sales talent, but who actually prize other considerations in hiring and retaining staff that do not foster a performance-driven culture. They express great frustration at the lack of productivity from their current team—only to revert to the safe and predictable hiring habits of old when faced with the unenviable prospect of parting with "old friends."

It might seem a tad obvious to assert that it serves little purpose in aspiring to have a sales team that drives performance—if you really would prefer to live in a harmonious environment where everyone gets along and nobody rocks the boat. That contradiction, however, is an all-too-common occurrence. As Robert Levin and Joseph Rosse wrote in *Talent Flow*, "Giving others bad news is never pleasant, so it is hard to imagine anyone actually enjoying firing an employee. It's easy though to see how you might be glad in retrospect to have the poor performer out of your unit's way. The problem is that the desire to avoid an uncomfortable short-term situation often wins out over the desire to solve the performance problem for the long term."

Only 4% of the 700 salespeople tested were *Hybrids*. These people had the drive and transaction orientation of a *Hunter* and also the patience and empathy of a *Farmer*. Hybrids not only have the urgency and drive to execute sales in the immediate term but they have the patience and empathy to develop relationships and to stay engaged with the customer through a longer sales cycle. *Hybrids*, I should point out, while they are the most desirable of profiles, are so difficult to find that it might be an exercise in frustration to attempt to identify and hire only this category of salesperson. A better approach is to fashion your sales team between *Hunters* and *Farmers* and to grab and keep any *Hybrids* that you might happen upon during your hiring and testing process if they meet your other criteria (culture fit, background checks, etc).

Hunters make up 13% of the 700 salespeople tested and, in many cases, they are the most difficult people to manage. They have a drive and a desire to close the sale immediately, and they can become quite impatient with the prospect if they believe the sale is not going to happen. This impatience and willingness to profile prospects can make *Hunters* very difficult to work with and their driving style sometimes results in customers becoming pressured and possibly offended, if they feel that they are being hurried along, passed over to another salesperson, or profiled right out of the store.

It is not unusual to see a *Hunter* give up on a customer very quickly if he feels that the customer is not ready to buy at that moment. This can result in some hurt feelings and, if the customer does not walk out of the store as a result of being ignored, they can occasionally buy from a *Farmer*, responding better to the more patient, more communicative style. As Rich Pesqueira said, "I still never believe customers when they say they want to think about it and come back another day. I think that instinct has served me pretty well and helped me close more sales on the first visit, but I'm sure I've alienated a couple of would-be customers along the way."

While *Hunters* have their shortcomings, there is no question that they are difference-makers. Their wiring to get it done now ensures that few opportunities are missed and there will always be activity and action when they are involved. As I mentioned earlier, my friends with stores in the Caribbean need to have a healthy supply of *Hunters* in their stores. For them, the ships dock for a few hours in port and they may have a mere few minutes with each prospect before they leave the store and the ship literally sails away. *Hunters* are clearly great asset s in high-traffic environments but they are also pretty important in slower-paced environments where every opportunity and every sale counts.

Farmers represented 25% of all salespeople who were tested and, while the style is more relationship-based and more patient, it would be a mistake to dismiss the value of *Farmers* in your store. They do have the capacity and the wiring to sell and they are capable of occasionally stepping up their pace to the *Hunter* level during the holiday season and for short periods of time when called upon. Their more friendly style also works for customers who may not respond well to the more high-pressure style of the *Hunter*. With one in four of the 700 testing out as *Farmers*, they make the second largest group (after *Wrong Business*) and they play a very important role on the sales team.

Accepting the huge and potentially futile challenge of attempting to find *Hybrids*, I would argue that a good ratio on a sales team ought to be two *Farmers* for every one *Hunter*. To reverse that ratio, and have twice as many *Hunters* as *Farmers*, might result in decidedly more drama on the sales floor than is acceptable and an environment that could be overly competitive and not as customer-friendly as you might like.

In short, what you should have is a very good balance of *Hunters* and *Farmers*. It would be great if you can find some *Hybrids* to build your team around but, as previously stated, they are very difficult to find. Wherever possible, and as soon as possible, find a way to minimize the number of *Wrong Business* people on your team, no matter how nice, pleasant and tenured they are. They are generally easy to manage, very low maintenance and highly unproductive.

No matter how your *Personnel Landscape* shapes out, it is very important that each member of the team knows exactly what their role is. Asking *Hunters* to be great *Farmers*, or asking *Farmers* to sustain a level of transactional performance more in keeping with a *Hunter's* performance is not a winning business strategy. Both types are valuable salespeople and ought to be used to the best of their own abilities and in a manner consistent with their inherent wiring.

The important thing is to have people on your team who are wired to be salespeople, whether they are *Hunters*, *Farmers* or *Hybrids*, and to put them in the best position to succeed.

The Up-System

"Hell, there are no rules here - we're trying to accomplish something."
Thomas Edison

I would be remiss if I didn't spend a little time talking about one of my great peeves in retail sales. The *Up-System* is perhaps one of the most inane of dictates on a retail sales floor. The basic premise of the system is that all salespeople are created equally and, as such, ought to have exactly the same number of opportunities to engage and close prospects. If we lived in a world where all salespeople were created equally the *Up-System* would be a nice way to ensure harmony. We might even select an appropriate musical score to accompany our efforts and all would be well—with happily fulfilled customers, delightfully pleasant and incredibly effective salespeople, and an orchestra of string instruments, maybe even a harp or two, to score this beautiful scene. Do you remember when we all had record players? This is where the needle scratches across the record, making an awful sound and bringing this fairytale to a grinding halt.

Alas, the world does not work that way. All salespeople are not created equally. Each interaction with a prospect affords your business a great opportunity to turn that prospect into a satisfied customer and the *Up-System* will ensure neither a harmonious work environment, nor a profitable or rewarding experience for any of the parties involved: you, your employees or, most importantly, your customers. The net effect of the *Up-System* is that your best salespeople will be denied the opportunity to do what they do best over and over again. Your prospects will be denied the best opportunity to satisfy their needs over and over again, and your store will be infinitely less successful and less profitable than it otherwise could be. As Eric Herrenkohl writes in *How To Hire A-Players*, "If you want to build an A-player team, you need to stop trying to turn poor performers into A-players and commit more time to finding and hiring A-players. Then, invest the same leadership and coaching time with them that you used to spend trying to fix your poor performers."

The best argument for the *Up-System* is that you want to give everyone the same opportunity to be successful, that you do not want to exacerbate the disparity that might already exist between your top performers and your under-performers, and that you do not want to create a culture so competitive that it negatively impacts the customer experience.

Let's address the two main arguments cited above: 1) the basic premise of fairness and 2) the customer experience. In the first instance, you will find that there is, and will likely always be, a variance in performance of your better salespeople when compared to that of your weaker salespeople. Those folks who are wired to sell will, with very few exceptions, always be at the top of the performance pyramid. Conversely, the salespeople who are generally amongst your lowest performers, on the whole, will always be your lowest performers.

Your best salespeople do a better job at converting prospects into customers. Those customers spend more per transaction than customers converted by your least successful salespeople. They are also more inclined to add on to their purchases and to lay the foundation for future purchases. Let's do a little basic math to understand the differences that can result from good performance versus mediocre performance.

If your best salespeople are converting three of every ten prospects into customers, and if their average sale is 20% higher than their less accomplished colleagues, you can see what impact that has on a very small sample of time. In this very conservative example, the resulting numbers would see your best salespeople performing at level that is 180% of their colleagues.

Prospects Converted of 100:	Average Sale:	Total:
Good Salespeople: 30	$120	$3,600
Weaker Salespeople: 20	$100	$2,000

To be fair, this is likely an overly conservative example. Your best people are probably converting prospects at a better clip than 30%. They are also potentially performing at a level that is beyond that extra 20% per transaction shown in the example above. The small and conservative sample shows a performance variable between your best salespeople and your weaker salespeople that when spread over a year might look like this:

- **Top Salesperson $720k**
- **Weaker salesperson $400k**

The difference in sales from the above scenario is actually quite conservative, as a top salesperson will often convert better than the 30% that I estimated. It might be a useful exercise for you to do the math in your own business. Compare your top performer with one of your weaker performers and see what the variation in sales performance is. We are often quick to dismiss the very significant differences in results from our top performers versus our weaker performers as just too complicated to understand. More profoundly, we allow ourselves to be seduced by thoughts of fixing the problem with training, coaching and/or compensation plan changes and we actually exacerbate the dysfunction by focusing our attention trying to fix the weaker performers instead of investing that precious time with your best performers.

The difference in performance is all about wiring, and that wiring manifests itself one prospect at a time, one sale at a time, one opportunity at a time. If you believe that you can train or incent wiring into someone who does not possess it, perhaps you might also consider giving "tall lessons" to short NBA aspirants.

When you look at the difference in performance from your top salesperson to one or more of those folks bringing up the rear I suspect that you will see that the aforementioned scenario is not only plausible but is, in fact, the very picture that your sales team paints on an ongoing basis. An *Up-System* does exactly what you intended it to do: it provides the same number of opportunities to close sales for all of your salespeople, regardless of their talent. The consequences of doing that are measured in significant lost sales and in dissatisfied customers and prospects.

The basic premise of why a prospect visits a retail store can and should be debated at length elsewhere. There are all sorts of theories as to why a person walks into your store, from those about retail therapy, killing time, aimless meandering, engaging in scouting work for some future important purchase, etc. Here's a thought, and it is the basic premise that ought to drive your culture, your hiring, your compensation plan and your training: a prospect always visits your store with the intention of buying something. I cannot be any more direct than that. Now, here's what might seem like a contradiction to you: I know that every prospect will not buy something every time he or she visits a store and I'm not trying to delude myself, or you, for that matter, into believing otherwise. What I am saying, as emphatically as I can, is that we must always act on the premise that this statement is true and by doing so we will be far more successful than if we believe otherwise. We must also communicate, consistently, and with emphasis, that this truth must govern the attitude and mindset of all of our salespeople. All customers who come into our store do so with the intention of buying something. Period. End of story! The facts will, of course, prove otherwise but that truth must govern our approach and our expectation. There are many reasons why this attitude needs to permeate:

> ➢ By believing that to be true we will adopt an entirely different approach to each and every customer interaction. We will bring into each prospect experience an expectation of actually selling something.

> ➢ We will send a very clear signal to our sales team that every single prospect visit presents a selling opportunity and that prospects who are not converted into customers are a missed opportunity.

> ➢ As owners/managers/principles of the stores you will better understand why more prospects need to be seen by top salespeople, the people who give you the best opportunity to convert prospects into customers.

> ➢ We best serve our prospects and customers by treating them as though they have chosen to visit our store to buy that day, even if they initially tell us otherwise.

This last point is as fundamental as any you are going to read in this book. Customers don't always tell us why they have come into our stores. Sometimes, they don't even know why they have come into our stores. Rich Pesqueira often says that the customer doesn't always know his lines and I couldn't agree more. Delivering a great experience and a great product solution to the customer is a win-win situation all around. There is a reason that great salespeople convert more prospects into customers and it has a lot to do with the fact that they conduct themselves as though every customer wants to buy that very day. They are not right 100% of the time, but they are right far more often than their less accomplished colleagues and the business and the customers are better for it. I will share a couple of personal experiences elsewhere in this book to demonstrate how buying decisions and non-buying decisions are made based on the attitude, mindset and approach of certain salespeople.

To close this segment, I will go back to Michael Jordan and the Chicago Bulls. Sports offer great metaphors for business and, as a Chicago Bulls fan, I can think of no better example to point out the futility of the *Up-System* than that 90s Bulls team. As a reminder, the Bulls won six NBA titles from 1991 to 1998. The Bulls had, during that eight-year period, two "three-peats" with two years in between without winning a title. During the six title wins, Michael Jordan played an amazing role, winning the most valuable player award in all six championships. In the two years that the Bulls did not win the NBA title in that eight-year span, Michael Jordan was absent for the first year, and for most of the second year—a consequence of his having quit basketball to try his hand at professional baseball.

Can you imagine what would happen if the Bulls coach, Phil Jackson, had implemented an *Up-System*? While I am not suggesting that your best salespeople rank as the retail equivalent of Michael Jordan, the idea, nonetheless, of taking your best player and giving her one of every five shots—while your role players take an equal number— is tantamount to having some of the lesser known Bulls from that era take the same amount of shots as Michael Jordan. When the game is on the line—and the game is on the line every single day in retail stores—we simply must have our best players taking the shots. With all due respect to Chuck Nevitt, Mark Randall, Ricky Blanton and Bob Hansen, etc. (all NBA title winners with the Bulls), the championships would likely never happen without the stars like Jordan and Scottie Pippen. Great teams cannot win without role players like Nevitt, Blanton, Randall and Hansen. They play a very key role in allowing the stars to do what they do best. They are not, however, expected to consistently take the important shots. Prospects are too important to your business and you must create a system that gets your best players in front of them as often as possible.

Conversion

Mark Ryski writes in *Conversion: The Last Great Retail Metric,* that retail sales can be boiled down to a very simple equation:

Traffic x Conversion x Average Sale

Ryski makes a very compelling argument, supported with interesting stories and data, that the conventional metrics used for decades to measure sales performance are outdated. In its most stripped down hypothesis, Ryski suggests, and I confess to sharing his view, that arbitrarily congratulating or admonishing sales teams for increases, decreases, or flat performance versus the prior year can be somewhat misleading if we are not measuring conversion.

For instance, if your store has a 10% increase in sales versus the same period for the prior year you might, particularly in a more challenging economic climate, view that performance as exceptionally good. On the other hand, if your performance was flat versus the previous year, you might lament your team's poor performance and implement potentially damaging changes to personnel, to your compensation plan, to your product mix, to you advertising, etc. Absent the context of conversion, you may find yourself lauding the appearance of great performance and criticizing the illusion of poor performance.

Let's use the same numbers and add the extra layer of conversion into the mix. What if I were to tell you that in the first instance (10% growth), you actually grew your traffic by 25%. Let's say that your marketing efforts were sufficiently exciting and resonant and it helped drive a significant increase in your foot traffic. Or, perhaps, an important new tenant came into the lifestyle mall where your store is located and it helped bring a lot more traffic into the store. Or maybe the road work project that seems to have taken forever to complete was finally finished, and customers can now more readily access your center and store. There are, of course, many reasons why traffic into your store might increase but no matter what the reason, it is important to understand the numbers in context.

In the 10% growth scenario, your team might have actually under-performed relative to the number of prospects they had to work with. They saw far more customers than the previous year and they converted far fewer of them into customers.

Let's run the numbers as if the store did $1.1m in the most recent year, up from $1m the previous year. In the interest of keeping the math very basic, let us assume a $250 average sale for each of the two years. That means your team successfully transacted 4,000 sales at $250 average sales in year one. In the most recent year, your team successfully transacted 4,400 transactions at $250 average sale. Those extra 400 transactions look pretty good, even as you might wish that your average sale had increased.

	Unit Sales	Average Per Ticket	Total Sales
Year One:	4,000	$250	$1,000,000
Year Two:	4,400	$250	$1,100,000

Now let's add in the conversion factor. What if you learned that the 4,000 successful transactions from year one resulted from 20,000 prospects (remember, you are measuring your foot traffic) and your 4,100 sales from year two were converted from 24,000 prospects? That would mean that in year one, your team converted 20% of all prospects into customers and in year two they converted just over 17% of your prospects into customers. You managed to drive more people into the store in the second year, but a higher percentage of those people walked out without making a purchase.

	Prospects:	Converted to a Sale:	Conversion Ratio:
Year One:	20,000	4,000	20%
Year Two:	24,000	4,000	17%

It is possible, of course, that there might have been important and damaging product issues that contributed to that performance; perhaps a previously best-selling brand or major product category is no longer hot, or is no longer available to you. You may have made some product choices (not replenishing best-sellers frequently enough, missing out on key price points, etc.) that had a negative impact on the team's ability to convert. You might, with the best of intentions, have changed the compensation plan, only to find that the new plan actually reinforced the wrong behaviors. You might have changed personnel or scheduling, unwittingly creating a situation where your most effective people were missing valuable prospects. In short, there are many reasons that might explain the decline in conversion but you can't address them unless you know that they exist in the first place.

In any case, you had better be looking at the conversion ratio to determine whether it is a one-off situation that can be explained and corrected or whether it is the beginning of a slide that could be very damaging to your business. In year one, 16,000 people walked out of your store without making a purchase. One can debate the merits of what the conversion ratio ought to be, but you should understand those raw numbers to help you understand where there might be room for improvement. In year two, 19,900 people walked out of your store without making a purchase. That's a 24.4% increase in the number of people that <u>did not</u> make a purchase over the previous year. Again, is it an explainable phenomenon or is it a disturbing trend?

	Total Prospects	Converted to a Sale	Not Converted to a Sale
Year One:	20,000	4,000	16,000
Year Two:	24,000	4,000	19,900

Now take the scenario where your sales were flat versus the prior year. How would you feel about that seemingly disappointing performance if you learned that your traffic was down 20% versus the same period the previous year? You now have a frame of reference that suggests what you did not know before. From underperforming, your sales team is actually doing a much better job than sales numbers alone would suggest. They have stepped up their performance by converting more prospects into customers from the considerably smaller base they had to work with.

In that scenario, the issue of no-growth may have a lot more to do with changes in your marketing efforts, or other to-be-determined factors, rather than from poor performance from your sales team. Another way to look at the "flat" performance is that in year one, 16,000 people walked out of your store empty-handed, while in year two—the seemingly disappointing year—12,000 people walked out of your store empty-handed. Your conversion rate went from 20% to 25% in the space of one year.

In theory, your conversation rate should go up as your traffic count declines. Fewer prospects coming into your store generally affords more time for your team to work with each customer. I deliberately said "in theory" because it doesn't always play out that way. A poorly constructed sales team is probably going to be just as anemic with fewer prospects as they are with more prospects. A quality team, on the other hand, will deliver the opposite result.

	Prospects:	Converted to a Sale:	Conversion Ratio:
Year One:	20,000	4,000	20%
Year Two:	16,000	4,000	25%

	Unit Sales	Average Per Ticket	Total Sales
Year One:	4,000	$250	$1,000,000
Year Two:	4,400	$250	$1,000,000

Again, for the purpose of keeping the math simple, the above scenario of flat sales, generally frowned upon by growth-minded managers, suggests that the sales team is significantly out-performing the previous year by converting one in four prospects into customers instead of the one in five converted from the previous year.

There are many tools available to retailers who want to measure conversion, from complex and sophisticated POS and camera systems to simple door-counters. No matter which system you choose, it is hard to imagine why any retail business would not want to measure foot traffic and conversion as central elements of your key performance indicators.

A last point on the matter of measuring traffic, I have heard many retailers dismiss the relevance of door-counters as they cannot distinguish a prospect from a customer from an employee from the UPS delivery man. That is correct; the most rudimentary door-counter cannot make that distinction, but it couldn't make that distinction last year either, so you are, to a large extent, measuring apples to apples. It doesn't so much matter that the numbers are right to a person as much as it matters that you understand more generally what your conversion rates look like from one year to the next. If your employees enter and exit through the same door as your customers, that skewing of the numbers should not materially impact the broader picture. And, while we're on the subject, make sure your team treats the UPS driver like a quality prospect too, because he is.

Up-selling/Cross-selling

I grew up in Ireland and Clarks was always considered to be a great brand of shoes in an era when brands were no quite the cultural imperative they are nowadays. One early summer day, I was shopping in the Fashion Mall in Las Vegas and I happened upon a Clarks store. I went into the store, perhaps to satisfy some nostalgic itch, and I began to putter about in the area of the store where they displayed their sandals.

I should mention that I have the ugliest feet in the world and I hate buying sandals, even though I enjoy wearing them in summer. Long hot summers, of course, are much more the rule in these parts, than in Ireland, and I have come to appreciate the comfort offered by a nice pair of sandals.

After perusing the selection for a few minutes, I liked a particular pair and I asked the salesman for my size so that I could try them on. To my absolute delight, I found that they fit beautifully, they concealed my ugly feet pretty well, while still allowing the freedom and openness of a traditional sandal—and they looked pretty good too. Needless to say, I produced my credit card and asked the salesman to "ring me up."

As we got to the POS terminal, the salesman suggested, without any hesitation and imbued with the confidence of expectation, that I should take the black sandals too. He was holding the brown sandals that I had tried on and he had heard me wax poetic about how I wished that I could wear sandals more often, but that I was overly sensitive about my ugly feet. It must have seemed like the most natural thing in the world for him to believe that I ought to have a pair in brown and in black. I thanked him for his welcome suggestion and I agreed to take the black sandals too.

I was very impressed with how intuitive that salesman was, and I have often thought about him since. He doubled his sale with that one suggestion and I was better served for his having taken that initiative and made the suggestion. I got to enjoy both pairs of sandals for quite a few years and I had no intention of even looking for sandals when I stopped into the store. If we were to consider the implications of his selling style, and the absolute ease with which he was able to double that transaction, one can only imagine how very productive he must be over the course of a year.

That experience is a great example of a salesperson not only asking for the sale, but of anticipating and expecting an up-sell. Great sales-people do that every single day, in most every transaction and, just like in my case, they are going to be successful some of the time, simply by asking for the sale. Think about the implications of him being success-ful even one or two times for every ten transactions. That's a 10 to 20% difference in sales. That can be the difference between a retail store being profitable and not being profitable over the course of a year.

Great salespeople always anticipate that there will be opportunities to add on to the sale. They don't stop and salute themselves for hav-ing successfully converted a prospect into a customer; they continue to explore any and all possibilities to continue to satisfy that customer. In my case, I was better served for having bought not just one but two pairs of sandals. You should create an expectation of add-on sales in your retail store. It is far from the pushy snake-oil salesman of old, pressuring people into buying things they do not need. It is just plain good business to respectfully and confidently explore opportunities to deliver even more value to a customer after an initial commitment. You never know, they just might like the black sandals too.

The Customer
Experience

"When given the choice of obsessing over competitors or obsessing over customers, we always obsess over customers." Jeff Bezos

In the 1980s, I was working as a retail salesperson for Tiffany & Co. in Chicago. One day in holiday season, as I was hustling from customer to customer, I noticed an older gentleman, very quietly, very patiently, waiting for someone to engage him. I made sure to make eye contact with him and I indicated that I would be with him momentarily. After I thanked the customer I had been helping, I turned back to the man and I recognized him as the singer/entertainer, Andy Williams.

Mr. Williams thanked me for acknowledging him and he mentioned that he had been unable to get a salesperson on the second floor to take care of him. He said that he had waited for quite some time and that not one of the salespeople had even acknowledged him, let along offered to wait on him. We were in the midst of the holiday season and, while it might have taken a little longer than usual to get to a waiting customer, there was, nonetheless, absolutely no excuse for Mr. Williams, or any other customer, to have waited so long without the basic courtesy of being acknowledged.

While it had not immediately occurred to me, later that day I was struck by how ironic it was that Andy Williams had found it so hard to get waited on at Tiffany & Co. At that stage, Tiffany had been around for about 150 years, and had carved quite a legacy for itself as a great icon of American retailing. An important brick in that iconic status was the notoriety that came from the wonderful film *Breakfast At Tiffany's,* based on the Truman Capote book and starring Audrey Hepburn and George Peppard.

The theme song from that great film is "Moon River," written by Henry Mancini and Johnny Mercer—and the song, which won an Academy Award in 1962, was sung by none other than Andy Williams. It became the song most closely associated with Andy Williams for the remainder of his career.

That Andy Williams, of "Moon River," of *Breakfast At Tiffany's,* could not get waited on at that iconic store was a very poignant reminder of how much work had to be done to more quickly, more appropriately, engage with our customers.

To suggest that great customer service is important is sort of like saying that breathing is a good idea to sustain life. Despite that immutable assertion, great service is, unfortunately, not the norm in retail stores. As a great admirer of top-notch service, I confess that I am far more often underwhelmed by the service I get than I am impressed. In fact, I might argue that those occasions when I do receive outstanding customer service are very much the exception.

There is something quite paradoxical about the service provided by top performers. They can appear, on occasion, to be very dismissive of prospects that they quickly deem to be less than worthy of their full attention (a fact not unnoticed by their less-accomplished colleagues, who will usually point these occasions out as evidence that they just wouldn't conduct themselves in that fashion...which, apparently, explains why they don't sell as much) and yet they seem to attain superhero status in what they will do for their own customers. When push comes to shove, the outstanding sales performers can be selective with respect to with whom, and for how long, they invest their time. Once they engage their customers, however, they tend to set a very, very high standard of engagement and service.

Without excusing the occasional and infrequent infractions from the best sales producers, providing outstanding customer service must be an imperative in every retail store. Having a salesperson engage face to face with a customer is one of the biggest advantages that brick-and-mortar retailers have over their internet competitors. To cede that advantage by failing to meet a high standard of customer service is unforgivable.

About thirteen years ago, I had a truly awful experience at a Best Buy store close to my home in the Boston area. I had attempted to return an item that cost $12 and the experience dealing with the various employees and managers at the store was so bad that I never went back to that store, or to any Best Buy, ever again. I had up to that point given just about every single dollar of my electronic purchases to that retailer, having been introduced to them some years earlier when I lived in Texas. You might reasonably say that I defaulted to Best Buy for just about anything they sold - a near-perfect situation for any retailer. For $12, they lost my business forever.

As Eddie Kay writes in *Thriving In The Shadow Of Giants*, "All things being equal, I'll buy at the cheapest place. As a retailer, it is up to you to be as unequal as you can."

Winners Need to be Hugged

Because star salespeople come across as being very assertive, because they have good self-confidence, because they seem to handle the rejection of missed sales, and because they tend to be self-starters, there is a misconception that they do not need positive feedback from their managers and owners. They may be the last people on your team to ask for positive reinforcement but make no mistake about it: great salespeople need hugs just as much as weaker sales performers. No matter how aware they are of their own performance and results, they still crave positive feedback. Star performers should be acknowledged privately and publically for their accomplishments. The feedback, however, needs be sincere and specific. General and broad-based kudos will be far less effective than sharing a specific story about how a great sale happened, or a particular example of exceptional customer service. While we are understandably quick to acknowledge success stories of people who are not star performers, and why wouldn't we want to celebrate the successes of our weaker players, we should not underestimate the positive effects of acknowledging the wins of our best salespeople. Bob Phibbs writes in *The Retail Doctor*, "Drivers will be the first to leave you, looking for someone who will appreciate them. Want to kill a Driver? Ignore him, take credit for his idea, or patronize him."

Training

"If I skip practice for one day, I notice. If I skip practice for two days, my wife notices. If I skip practice for three days, the world notices." Vladimir Horowitz

I have on occasion been accused of dismissing the relevance of sales training. The criticism, perhaps understandably, derives from my resistance to view sales training as a solution to poor sales performance. Let me be very clear so that there is no misunderstanding my position on the issue. Training will not fix a sales performance problem if that problem is related to poor sales wiring. If you have hired people to perform in a sales job, who do not possess the natural wiring to be salespeople, no amount of training will change them.

I have seen it over and over through the years: retail managers and owners spending time, energy and money attempting to turn non-producing salespeople into productive salespeople. It doesn't work. And, on the rare occasions when the training appears to have been effective, I will offer the following sage advice: stick around, it won't sustain. People who do not have the wiring for sales will, sooner rather than later, revert to their comfort levels and any benefits from the training will quickly dissipate.

Sales training dollars are best spent on people who have the fundamental wiring to be salespeople. You will see a beautiful irony when sales training is invested in real salespeople; they tend to soak up the learning as though they were starting from scratch and hearing everything for the first time. They are looking for style tips, interesting language, nuances and reflections, anything to give them an advantage.

I attended a Human Resource conference in Philadelphia a couple of years ago and I noticed something very different from the many sales training meetings and conferences I had previously attended. In the HR conference, the room filled up from the back to the front. In the many sales conferences I have participated in, not only did the room fill up from the front to the back, but the best, most recognizable salespeople, always seemed to find themselves in the front seats.

A cynic might suggest that salespeople just want to be front and center in the room, or always the center of attention, etc. While there might be some element of truth in that for some of them, the reality is they want to learn and to grow. They want to become better salespeople and to somehow find an edge. I have very often found myself standing in front of the best salespeople, wondering if they are hearing anything that they have not heard before, or that they don't intuitively know and yet they seem to be consuming every word and they are present, physically, intellectually and emotionally.

Steve Suggs writes in *Can They Sell*, "Product training, face-to-face sales skills and motivational training are three separate and distinct types of training. The best salespeople are always investing time and money in all three areas. They read books, listen to audio training, attend seminars, hire personal coaches, and attend company conventions. They are always learning and feeding their minds with positive affirmations."

If you find yourself at a sales conference and you want to find the non-sales producers, start working your way to the back of the room. That's where you will typically find the better note-takers, perhaps even some of the better learners. What you are not likely to see are the real sales drivers. They'll be occupying the seats closest to the speaker and they will likely be hanging on her every word. Training is and will always be essential, not just for the obvious reasons of equipping your best people with the requisite knowledge of your products and services, etc., but because your very best salespeople expect you to make that investment in them. In many respects, they see it as an important element of your promise (spoken or otherwise) to them to provide an engaging and aspirational environment.

In *First Break All The Rules*, Buckingham and Coffman write, "Here we come to one of the most profound insights shared by great managers, skills, knowledge, and talents are distinct elements of a person's performance. The distinction among the three is that skills and knowledge can easily be taught, whereas talents cannot. Combined in the same person, they create an enormously potent compound but you must never confuse talents with skills and knowledge. If you do, you may waste a great deal of time and money trying to teach something that is fundamentally unteachable." Training is much too important to waste on the wrong people.

The Job Description

The job description is one of the most important elements in the talent acquisition process and it is all too often very poorly served. It is crucial to get the job description right and yet we very often see job postings that are nothing if not a laundry list of requirements, without any real sense of clarity or prioritization, to the extent that it is almost impossible to decipher what the employer is really looking for. This tendency to list everything that you would like to see in a candidate can work against your best interests. It is much more effective to focus on the central elements of the position so that the reader is left in no doubt as to what the most important aspects of the job really are. Ambiguous language such as "friendly, customer-oriented, attention to detail and a team player" does little to establish a hierarchy of needs. As Eric Herrenkohl writes in *How To Hire A-Players*, "If you don't understand what the job requires, it's impossible to determine if someone is right for the role."

One of the best exercises in helping to write an effective job description is to profile your best people. First of all, you will pick the very best characteristics of those top performers, the factors that are the real difference-makers and which make them so successful in sales. In the second instance, in modeling your top people, you will be forced to accept that your best people come with flaws and shortcomings. Factors that do not inhibit their performance should not figure into your job description. There are "nice-to-haves" and there are "must-haves."

A job description is not intended to be a comprehensive manifesto of everything you would like to see in an applicant. For instance, you would not put into a job description that the successful candidate must show up to work on time every day, that she should dress appropriately, that she cannot engage in harassing behavior of her colleagues, etc. You would not likely suggest—although I have seen it done on many occasions—that the candidate must have great integrity. Is someone without great integrity actually going to read that and exclude themselves from the application process?

The job description should be as specific as possible, as brief as it can be—and with a clear hierarchy of needs/desires. Your first priority is to communicate the most important attributes of the job, not every conceivable quality that you might like. Anders writes in *The Rare Find*, "It's unnerving how many talent hunts go astray because no one makes a brave, clear-headed call about what the job really requires."

A focused and purposeful job description should serve as a filter to weed out candidates who are clearly not interested but who otherwise might be captured by a net that is cast too wide. The job description should resonate with candidates that you would really like to connect with, because the specificity of the job description speaks to them directly. The interview process will provide the best opportunity to determine whether there are important factors not listed in the job description that you need to further explore.

The following is a posting that I took from a popular job board. It is fairly typical and it is neither specific, nor particularly enlightening:

"We are in need of an organized and creative person to work closely with the owner of a custom high end jewelry and fine craft retail business on a daily basis. We are looking for an organized and creative person to do sales, display, bookkeeping and office work, manage website / marketing/ social media, and run errands as needed; must be able to adapt with the changing needs of the business. Some knowledge of jewelry materials and an interest in handmade art is required. We are willing to train but the ideal person will have good computer /office / people / sales skills and be able to work in a fast

paced creative environment. This is a full time position (five days including Saturdays) and the pay is commensurate with the amount of experience."

If you break that laundry list down into its most basic requirements, it asks for:

- Organizational skills
- Creativity
- Sales skills
- Display talent
- Bookkeeping
- Office Work
- Website Management
- Marketing
- Social Media
- Run errands
- Good Computer Skills
- People Skills

I think you will agree that it would be nearly impossible to understand what that job is about. The laundry list covers almost everything except making lunch for the owner and, all humor aside, that might fall under the "Run Errands" requirement. Look, this owner may be saying that he needs a jack-of-all-trades to help him in his small business. If that is the case, spell that out but put the small amount of absolutely must-haves on the posting. The above list is comprehensive to the point that it is meaningless and I can't imagine what kind of applicants it could possibly attract, beyond people who are throwing resumes at the wall hoping that one will stick. If sales is not the most important thing then take it off. Does he really need to list "run errands as needed"? What does "creative" mean to this business? Again, focus on the most important attributes and you can talk about some of the other things you would like to have during the interview.

Here's another posting from the same job site:

"We are now accepting applications for full-time Sales Professionals in our Fine Apparel and Better Apparel departments. Candidates must be self-motivated, have strong customer skills and the desire to succeed in a commission environment. Luxury retail experience preferred."

This posting is very specific in what it requires and it delivers infinitely more clarity and directness by saying less. If we break this posting down into its core requirements, here is what it asks for:

- Self-motivated
- Strong customer skills
- Desire to succeed in a commission environment
- Luxury retail experience preferred

Reasonable people can assume that the company above will require that successful candidates have great personal integrity, that they dress appropriately for the environment, that they have a comfort level reaching out to customers to generate business, etc. We can assume that they require that their applicants have a strong work ethic and that they will show up for work on time. Those are reasonable assumptions and they do not need to be listed in the job posting. What they have clearly communicated, however, is that this is a luxury retail world that requires their people to be comfortable driving business and providing a great customer experience in that environment.

In writing a job posting you need to be as specific as possible. Avoid the tendency to list everything that you would like and focus on the most important attributes of the job. Think about what you most love about your most successful salesperson right now, or someone who used to work for you. If you had to sum up what their most admirable attributes are, what would that look like? If you were to list those attributes in four or five bullet points, what would that look like? The more you say in your posting, the less you will communicate.

The Interview Process

The extent to which the interview process will be successful will always be commensurate with the level of preparation done in advance. This is neither the time nor the place to 'trust your gut' or your 'great people skills.' Success in the interview process can be boiled down to three elements:

1. You have hired a salesperson that will likely be a good fit.
2. You have eliminated candidates who would likely not have been a good fit.
3. You have <u>not</u> eliminated candidates who might be a good fit.

If you deem an interview to have been successful because it resulted in a hire, what would you think, with the benefit of hindsight, if you realized that you made the wrong hire? Was the interview successful or not? You obviously believed that you made the right hire at the time but you later realized that it was a bad hire. It is possible to have a great interview and for the fit to ultimately be wrong. With the best of intentions, you might have done a great job in preparing for the interview, doing your due diligence and executing a good interview. Unfortunately, it is far more likely that you thought the interview was great, because it resulted in a hire decision when, in fact, a more diligent process would have ruled out the candidate. It just might take you many months or even years, to realize that the interview was not successful.

It is not possible to have a good interview that results in a bad hire. If you have made a bad hire, than you probably failed to do your due diligence in advance of the interview and you likely failed to do a good enough job during the interviewing itself. Too many employers lament the outcome of bad hires as just bad luck and that self-delusion comes at a very heavy price. At the other end of the spectrum, you will never know the loss from an interview that missed a great talent, also a bust.

Remember, as obvious as it may seem, a successful interview does not mean that you have necessarily hired someone; it means that the process of uncovering whether the candidate will be a good fit or not was effective and that you ultimately made the right decision for your company.

With the exception of bringing entirely too much weight to bear on hiring experienced candidates, the single biggest reason that we fail at interviews is because of our inherent personal biases. Protest all you must, and pretend that you are the exception, but it happens in the vast majority of cases and, I hate to say, it is completely understandable.

It is human nature to instinctively respond positively or negatively to people when we first meet them. There is an immediate impression that forms in our subconscious the moment we meet a new person, shake a hand, lay eyes on his or her outfit and hairstyle, etc. From that first split second, we have a tendency to marry our biases and the die will have been cast for the duration of the meeting. Willis and Todorov wrote, "People rarely revise their first impressions; they just become more confident that they are right."

Having established our initial impressions so incredibly fast, we are now at the mercy of our ego, which happily sets off on its own journey to reinforce those initial impressions and prove to ourselves how brilliantly insightful we are. Have you ever heard anyone boast about how great their instincts for people are? Have you yourself ever made such a claim? It is human nature to believe that we have a marvelous capacity and instinct for "getting people," but it is folly to pursue that instinct as a hiring strategy. The interview process should be designed to explore and uncover three basic tenets of fit:

> ➤ **Culture**
> ➤ **Resume** (academic and/or professional)
> ➤ **Wiring**

I can't stress enough that being prepared for the interview is absolutely critical. Have your questions written out in advance and separate them into each of the three categories. Since this book is about uncovering the wiring of candidates, with and without experience, we will explore those questions in great detail in later chapters. With respect to resume and culture, I will also include a few questions that might be helpful to the interviewer. First, let us examine a few key pointers for the interview process.

A Place Without Interruptions

Interviewing on the fly, or in an environment where you are being interrupted by people and/or ringing telephones, is a bad way to operate. It is highly disrespectful to the candidate and it is counterproductive to your best interests. It is very unlikely, in the face of constant interruptions, that you will give the appropriate time and attention to the process, resulting in hiring, or not hiring, mistakes.

Interviewing prospective new hires is one of the most important things you do in your business and it ought to be prioritized and respected. Make sure the candidate is comfortable; offer her a glass of water and give your time and attention to her and to the interview process. Ask that you not be interrupted by calls or other people until the interview has concluded.

Remember, respecting the candidate in the interview process communicates to them the kind of person that you are and the kind of company you run. It will also go a long way towards determining whether a candidate that you deem worthy feels the same way about you and your business.

Some interviewers choose to sit behind a desk when they are interviewing; others prefer to sit across from the candidate, with a desk in between. I prefer to sit without the desk in between so that I don't create a metaphorical barrier between me and the candidate.

One significant benefit of sitting without the desk between you is that you can more easily observe the candidate's body language. I'll talk more about that later on.

One last note on creating a comfortable environment, I would always provide a glass of water for the candidate. Many candidates politely refuse the offer, only to find themselves desperately craving it as you both get deeper into the interview. That potential distraction can be so easily overcome by providing a glass at the outset.

Two Interviewers

I am a big fan of using two people to interview each candidate. This is especially true, but not exclusively so, when the interviewer is not a seasoned or trained human resource professional. I have found that mixing the dynamic with two people interviewing creates a more vibrant exchange, enables the interviewers to listen more carefully to each answer and allows the interviewer who is not asking the question to better observe the candidate's body language. With two interviewers, it is also easier to not let the candidate, or the interviewer, get into a groove such that the process of discovery gives way to a sort of mutual fan fest. It is important to keep things on message and to go back and forth on different topics so as to not get into too much of a flow. This is a counterintuitive as we typically want flow in social situations. Much as we enjoy "getting along" with new people, we want to be able to ask tough questions and we need to maintain enough objectivity to recognize when something doesn't feel or sound right.

The interviewing process works better when each interviewer has their own set of questions and the conversation continually shifts back and forth between the two interviewers. I would also encourage each interviewer to restate or rephrase a question previously asked by themselves or their colleague if they feel that the candidate has misunderstood or deflected the question. Croner and Abraham write in *Never Hire A Bad Salesperson Again*, "It is absolutely critical that we, not the interviewer, control the interview."

Be Prepared

Make sure that you have thoroughly gone over the resume and that you have a prepared list of questions to enable you to understand the important changes, developments, setbacks and accomplishments during the candidate's career to date. You should have a specific set of questions that address each of the three important areas:

> ➤ **Culture**
> ➤ **Resume**
> ➤ **Wiring**

I would suggest that you mix the questions as you discuss the three different areas. That will ensure that you don't allow the candidate to get into a pattern of responses dictated by any one area of discussion and it will keep him on his toes by requiring a thoughtful and specific response to each individual question.

While I am a staunch advocate of hiring salespeople with no previous sales experience, we still want to understand the progression of the candidate's career choices (or otherwise) to see if there are any issues that you ought to be concerned with. If there are unexplained gaps in the resume, they will need to be explained. Likewise, if there are specific accomplishments listed, they will make for good conversation, as the candidate explains how they accomplished the stated results. It has been my experience that the career objective stated at the top of the resume reveals a great deal. First of all, it should tell you what the real aspiration of the candidate is and that can be sometimes at odds with the job you are interviewing for.

Smart candidates will reshape their resume, especially the opening paragraph, to speak to the job that they are applying for. While their initiative in doing that is admirable, it highlights the need to explore whether he is a good fit or just a good interviewer. Focus on open-ended questions that encourage the candidate to give you specific response to accomplishments listed on his resume. Questions such as, "You said that you grew sales by 20% in your first year. Tell me how you did that."

Or, "You indicated that you grew sales by 15% but you were only in the job for eight months. Tell me how that worked."

Have a separate list of questions prepared that speak to your culture. These questions should explore whether the candidate is a good fit culturally, as distinct from the wiring questions or her resume exploration. The questions should serve to communicate some of the most important elements of your culture to the candidate, so that she can decide whether the company is a good fit for her. If the culture fit is not right nobody wins, as the employee will end up leaving or being terminated. The very best and most capable of candidates can run aground if they are not aligned with what the organization values and needs.

If you have not already done so, it would be a very good idea to list the essential elements of your culture and post them for your candidates and employees to see. This is a good way to establish the things that you value and which you expect your people to embrace.

I have had many store owners tell me that they themselves struggle to understand the unique aspects of their own culture. They can readily come up with the usual platitudes: "We treat our customers and our employees like family." "We're not a pushy environment; we give great service," etc, but they can't really expand beyond that.

Stores are all different and it is important to understand what is unique, and how those unique characteristics might impact employees, positively or negatively. Your store might be a very casual, laid-back environment with a sales team to match. Bringing a high-energy, vivacious, self-starter into an environment like that might be upsetting to the team and wholly unsatisfactory to the new hire, who may find such an environment to be an energy drain.

One fun way to capture some of the unique characteristics of your store is to have a fun pizza and beer (or wine) party and have your team discuss, debate and offer what they think makes your culture different and unique. It could be any number of things including the music you play on your sound system, the fact that you bake cookies to create a great aroma in your store, the particular way you greet your customers, the fact that you have family members working in the business, etc.

One of the biggest questions that must be addressed is whether your culture, by any reasonable definition, could reasonably be described as a "performance culture." If you do not like to set goals, if you do not hold your sales team accountable for sales performance (remember that "we don't like to be pushy with our customers" bit?), then you will have a hard time getting a high producer to fit in.

Once you have established and posted that list, you would be well served to construct a number of specific questions to establish culture fit. I have listed a number of sample questions that could be asked, but I would suggest that you compile some very specific questions that speak directly to your store's unique culture. Refrain from "selling" your culture to the candidate. You will be better served by asking the candidate questions to determine what makes the most sense for them and then see if that aligns with your environment, not the other way around.

There are obviously a myriad of questions that can be asked in order to assess culture fit. Make sure to include questions that get to the heart of those things that you most value in your organization.

If the new hire actually signals a change in priorities for your company (if you are looking to create a more competitive environment with greater sales accountability) and he or she is being hired as the "new breed" of salesperson in your company, you need to ensure that there is crystal clear communication to the rest of the team that the expectations are changing. A new hire can serve as a catalyst to lead change to a more performance-based culture but she and the team need to know that that is the direction you are taking the company and that she has your full support.

It is not at all unusual in a situation as described above for one or more of your current employees to overtly or covertly seek to undermine the new person. He or she may find fault at every opportunity and lead a campaign to discredit the new salesperson in order to avoid the transparency and accountability that will come when a new hire begins to outperform more seasoned salespeople. This insidious behavior, coupled with the fact that many top-performing salespeople come with a certain amount of baggage anyway, can be very destructive and can very often challenge even the most committed of owners, managers and new hires.

If you want to change to a more performance-based culture, but you insist on an orderly and harmonious transition, you may have difficulty getting there. You are effectively signaling to the current team that there is a new marshal in town, that the rules have changed and that they may not fit the bill anymore. That may be a very difficult pill to swallow for existing team members and it will require a steely resolve to manage through it.

We will look at the wiring questions, the most important and most difficult area of exploration and the biggest banana skin, later in the book.

Select Questions to Determine Culture Fit

> **Do you prefer to work independently or to work in a team? Discuss...**

> **Do you respond better to a base salary package or per formance-based compensation? Discuss...**

> **Would you describe yourself as a self-starter or do you like hands-on management?**

> **What do you like best about the culture in your current or last job?**

> **What do you like least about the culture in your current or last job?**

> **Describe the best boss you ever had...**

> **Describe the worst boss you ever had...**

Open-ended Questions

Whenever possible ask open-ended questions. Questions that begin with "Tell me about..." or "How did you accomplish..." or "What kinds of things did you do to..." are better than closed questions that don't reveal very much about the candidate. If you have need to ask some closed-ended questions, it is not unreasonable to assume that someone seeking a sales position ought to be able to offer a concise and relevant response that goes beyond a yes or no answer. Great salespeople are generally great storytellers and if you find yourself drowning in one-word answers, you are probably not looking at a great salesperson. Conversely, you do not want a storyteller to control and consume the entire interview.

In preparing for the interview, it is a good idea to write out the questions in advance and to shape as many of them as necessary as open-ended. There will, of course, be occasions when a simple yes or no answer will suffice but the more you can get the candidate to tell you how they did what they did (or what they say they did) the more you will learn about their capabilities.

Listen, Listen and Listen Some More

One of the best ways to dilute the impact of an interview is to talk too much. Prepare your questions, ask them and listen for the answers, without interruption. If the candidate has difficulty understanding the question, rephrase it for clarity and allow the candidate to answer it. Refrain from bullying or browbeating the candidate in the interview process—this is not supposed to be an interrogation—but be direct and unapologetically ask the questions you have prepared.

You will occasionally find that a candidate wants to take your question in another direction entirely to shape the response in his or her favor. Don't hesitate in situations like that to tell the candidate that you are interested in hearing their response to the question that you asked and politely restate the question. If you still cannot get a direct answer there is probably a good reason for the candidate's evasiveness and you might want to further explore the topic or question at that point, or later in the interview.

While western countries tend to frown on silence in social situations, do not be afraid of it when you are interviewing. Be respectful, be direct, ask the question and allow the candidate to answer it. Do not answer the question for the candidate. As crazy as that sounds, you would be shocked at how often we ask a question and then, unintentionally, lead the candidate to the answer we are looking for.

Body Language

It is not necessary to be an expert at reading body language to successfully interview sales candidates but it certainly helps if you have a basic working knowledge of things to watch for. Any perceived infraction in and of itself should be taken in context, but if you sense a level of discomfort on the whole, or when particular topics are being discussed, it might suggest a need for further exploration.

You should always expect the candidate to be somewhat nervous, in some case perhaps even very nervous, when you begin the interview process. No matter how confident the candidate appears, it is not at all unreasonable to allow for some early-interview jitters. That is one of the best reasons for making sure that the candidate is comfortably seated, that he or she has a glass of water at their fingertips (Note: don't ask the candidate if they want water, just get a water and put it in front of them). This nervousness is perfectly understandable and should not be viewed negatively. A minute or two of small talk and a relaxed, yet professional, mood can help to alleviate some of the nervousness prior to immersing yourself into the formal portion of the interview.

Once the interview commences, you must pay close attention to the candidate's body language. As I said, you don't have to be an expert at reading body language to know when a question or topic is making a candidate uncomfortable and, at a minimum you should continue to explore that question or topic to better understand why the candidate is displaying discomfort in addressing it. Observing body language can and should be done even in a one-on-one interview, but it is generally much easier to do if there are two interviewers.

The biggest giveaway that there is a level of discomfort about a topic or question is if the candidate's demeanor changes very significantly from what it had been prior to the question or topic being discussed.

Joe Navarro writes in *What Every Body Is Saying,* "We show discomfort when we do not like what is happening to us, when we do not like what we are seeing or hearing, or when we are compelled to talk about things we would prefer to keep hidden."

It is very important to note that body language stressors are not always a sign of dishonesty. It may be that the interviewer simply hadn't given much thought to what you are now asking about and the question may simply have induced a little anxiety. It may be that the topic or question touched a nerve about something totally unrelated, creating a momentary discomfort. Then again, the question may strike a nerve by touching on a subject that the candidate was hoping to avoid. It may open up a line of questioning about a blind spot or an experience that was previously kept buried. It may be that the candidate is experiencing some anxiety over a given question as it ignites stressors connected to a bad experience, strained workplace relationships, or professional or academic disappointments or failures.

The signs of discomfort should alert us to the likelihood that there is something beneath the surface that warrants further discussion, not necessarily that the candidate is being untruthful. In some instances, it might be worth delving a little deeper at the time you sense the stressors. There may also be a good reason to continue with your interview as planned and then return to the topic at a later time. By revisiting an uncomfortable situation later in the interview, you will get to see if the shift in body language you noticed earlier repeats itself—a potential red flag.

Some signs of body language stressors might include a candidate rubbing his hands up and down his legs, or crossing his arms across his chest. Sudden eye-fluttering is another sign, as are locked ankles. We might also look for hands that are tightly clenched. Another discomfort sign is a candidate that has his or her hands up around their own neck area (he's constantly adjusting his tie, she is rubbing her neck). Again, the most important tell is when there is a noticeable change in body language from where it had been just prior to the question or topic and, while the discomfort needs to be better understood, it does not by itself mean that the candidate is being untruthful.

If you have noticed stressors, there is nothing wrong with being very direct in asking the candidate why a given question seems to make them uncomfortable. You may get a very understandable explanation that will put your mind at ease. Then again, you may confirm that there was genuine discomfort and a costly bad hire was avoided.

Subjects that might illicit discomfort might include whether the candidate did, in fact, drive the sales increases as indicated on his or her resume. If you notice a shift in demeanor as you probe that matter, continue to dig deeper, or come back to it later in the interview. You might do the same if the candidate answered your enquiry about his relationship with his former boss by shifting uncomfortably in his seat and playing with the knot of his tie. That might be a perfect time to ask him what his boss would say about him if you were to call him.

Again, there is no need to take body language courses, or to read extensively on the subject (although either or both might be fun) to be an effective interviewer, but you should always pay attention to sudden shifts in a candidate's demeanor, particularly when it is related to a specific topic and especially when there is a pattern of discomfort whenever certain topics are probed. I'll leave the final word on this matter to David Lieberman in *You Can Read Anyone*: "Whenever you are faced with dual messages, here is the rule of thumb: trust emotional displays over the spoken word. Any time a physical gesture, facial expression, or words are incongruent, you can be fairly sure that what this presentation says is different from what he believes."

Resume Exploration

"When it comes to the past, everyone writes fiction." Stephen King

I will leave more expansive explanations of what one needs to do to fully vet and explore the candidate's resume to others. What I will say, however, is that you simply must understand two very important things about the resume when you do your homework; is it *real* and is it *relevant*?

A resume is a document that is put together to paint the most flattering picture of a candidate, sometimes without a modicum of objectivity. The candidate is inclined, almost compelled, to shape his or her story in a way that minimizes, and possibly even eliminates, shortcomings and highlights and exaggerates accomplishments. Accepting that as reality will help you to prepare the necessary questions to uncover what is real and what is relevant.

In doing your due diligence, look for unexplained gaps in employment and be respectful yet assertive in asking the candidate to explain those gaps. Sometimes there is a perfectly logical explanation for gaps. Look for anomalies, such as job shifts that do not seem like natural career progressions, moves that seem to have taken the candidate into an entirely different direction, choices that appear to be inconsistent with the stated career aspirations.

In an ideal world, there would be a natural career progression that is entirely consistent with the candidate's narrative and his stated objective. Unfortunately, we don't live in an ideal world and you will likely need to have some conversations about jobs that just didn't work out for one reason or another. Occasional deviations on a resume provide a great opportunity to engage the candidate in a meaningful and, hopefully, honest conversation that can get beneath the veneer of a typical resume track. It can give you an opportunity to see how the candidate handled failure, rejection and disappointment—all very important information to know.

Ask direct and open-ended questions about stated accomplishments and career highlights, questions such as "Tell me how you delivered that 20% year-over-year result" or "What specific things did you do to build that great sales team?" or "Tell me what types of things you did to build that client book."

I was once in a courthouse and heard a judge refer to a defendant's litany of lies as "padding his resume." Okay, that judge abused the daylights out of his judicial privilege but we get the sentiment. I'm okay with a candidate "rounding out the sharp corners" of his or her resume, but I have no tolerance for lies, lies and more damn lies. The resume should be an accurate reflection of where the candidate has come from and what he has done, with key highlights and achievements noted. To the best of the candidate's ability it should reflect accurate dates, titles and accomplishments. The vast majority of resumes offer a wealth of discussion topics if the interviewer is willing to put in the work in advance.

When I review a resume, I take a highlighter and I mark it up with things that I want the candidate to speak to. I want her to tell me how she did what she says she did and it is in the story that I decide how real it feels and whether there is a deeper learning about her inherent wiring and/or motivations that come from her answers.

The second thing that we must deduce from the resume is whether it is relevant or not. Since I am such a strong advocate of hiring salespeople with no previous experience, you might ask where the relevance is coming from. There are two basic elements I would look for, even with an inexperienced candidate:

> ➤ **Does the previous work and/or academic experience suggest a skill set, or character traits, that might be consistent with the wiring that is necessary for sales?**

> ➤ **Does the resume portray such a contradictory path as to suggest your job opening might be just one more temporary stop along the way?**

A resume that shows a candidate jumping from job to job over the course of their career ought to be viewed with some caution. The standard on this particular issue has understandably, and perhaps justifiably, relaxed in recent years, but constant changing, without any extended period of time in any given job, should at least warrant a direct conversation on the topic. Ask the candidate to help you to understand why there appears to be a pattern of job-hopping throughout their career. There may be a perfectly logical explanation. Then again, there may be an underlying root cause, such as an inability to get along with colleagues and/or supervisors, a chronic tardiness problem that ultimately wears thin, or even a problem with dishonesty or theft. We live in a world where few people expect or get a gold watch for extended service anymore. In an era where loyalty seems to be in ever shorter supply on both the employer and the employee side, resumes are more apt to show variety over tenure. While the stigma of multiple jobs may have abated, the need to explore why the candidate moved and how those moves aligned with their stated career aspirations is still as important as ever.

While it is not unusual to see gaps in employment, they need to be discussed to ensure that there is no back-story. Beyond some obvious reasons for gaps in employment such as maternity, tending to ailing family members, pursuing additional educational opportunities, traveling, etc., gaps in employment might also indicate a desire to keep a particularly unflattering professional or personal situation under wraps. Ask the candidate to explain the gaps in employment and ask him if he feels confident that the dates of employment listed on the resume are accurate. Watch the body language as you ask these important questions and probe as deeply as you need to if you do not feel comfortable with the answers provided.

Resumes that have a summary paragraph can communicate a great deal in those few short lines. You might be surprised how few people rewrite the executive summary specifically for each interview (which they really ought to do to ensure that it aligns with the needs of the position they are interviewing for) so, in a nutshell, you can learn a lot about how the candidate sees himself and what his priorities are. That is particularly helpful insofar as it will either reinforce what you heard from the candidate during the interview, or it will be at odds with what you heard.

If the summary aligns with the candidate's narrative regarding aspirations, skills, etc., that is obviously a good sign. If, on the other hand, what you hear throughout the course of the interview is not the same as the summary, it is fair game to ask the candidate why he is interviewing for a job that is inconsistent with his stated objectives.

The last point I will make about resumes is to look at the bottom to see if the candidate has listed his hobbies and interests. If you are looking for a highly driven salesperson you might be pleased to see hobbies and activities that are competitive and social in nature.

Compensation

I have listened to scores of managers over the years talking about their well-intentioned, but generally fruitless efforts to devise the perfect compensation system to help fix underperforming sales teams. Some managers choose to pay a higher base salary and no commission. They argue that removing the stress that comes from a performance-based compensation system has the effect of taking unnecessary pressure off their employees, thus allowing them to perform better.

Other managers choose to fashion a balance between base salary and commission. This, they believe, rewards stellar performance while still offering the stability of a predictable wage. Still others shape a compensation plan that is *all* about performance, believing a system that rewards the top performers *and* challenges lesser performers is the right way to go.

While there are few hard and fast rules about the perfect compensation system, what I will suggest is that any system implemented should favor the best performers. It should, to quote a wise sage, focus on the critical few, not the insignificant many. Compensation systems that attempt to counteract a bad hiring culture, by definition, will fail. You need to have a compensation system that rewards your very best performers. Top salespeople are not motivated by money alone, but they do need to be compensated in a manner commensurate with their stellar performance. They need to know that whatever system you have in place rewards their accomplishments over their less-successful colleagues. It doesn't really matter how the compensation is shaped as long as the scorecard, in the final analysis, shows the real movers and shakers at the top of the list. Anything less is a temporary residency for the best people until they find a more suitable place of employment.

If the message has not resonated strongly enough by now, I will tell you again that there is no compensation plan that will turn a horse into a squirrel. You may see temporary improvements, as a consequence of a new commission system or bonus plan, but the best performers, those with the inherent wiring for sales, will continue to be the best performers, and those who are not wired to make their living in sales will always bring up the rear.

You must pay your top performers enough to take the issue of money off the table. No matter what your compensation plan looks like, the goal should be that it serves as a meritocracy. Those salespeople who perform the best ought to be paid the most. And those folks who do not perform ought to have no entitlement to a compensation plan that rewards mediocrity.

Rob Dobelli wrote in *The Art of Thinking,* "In Ancient Rome, engineers were made to stand underneath the construction of their bridge's opening ceremonies. Poor incentive systems, on the other hand, overlook and sometimes even pervert the underlying aim." Salespeople, good and bad, ought to be made to stand underneath their bridges, to reap the rewards of their endeavors or to pay the price for their poor performance. How you construct your compensation plan is open to interpretation. That the plan be based on meritocracy should be immutable.

Motivation

Lou Holtz, the former Notre Dame football coach, once said, "Motivation is simple. You eliminate those who are not motivated." I laughed aloud when I first read Holtz's quote because of its directness and clarity and, quite frankly, its honesty. I could not imagine a more succinct assessment of this much discussed topic and because, as is often the case with quotes we are drawn to, I could not agree with it any more forcefully.

Rivers of ink and billions of digital impressions have been expended on the topic of motivation. No matter what business you are in, and most certainly in sales, sports and other competitive endeavors, we are constantly asking ourselves how we can motivate our teams, our underperformers, our potential superstars. To echo Mr. Holtz's sentiment, here's a thought: hire people who are already motivated to do the job you want them to do. I should throw in a very heartfelt word of caution here: that does not mean hiring people who demonstrate great motivation to get the job, to win you over during the interview, to pass the pre-employment process with flying colors but who are not really motivated to sell.

To reiterate, our job is to find people who are motivated to do the job, not people who motivated to impress during the interview process. In their seminal book, *How To Hire And Develop Your Next Top Performer*, Greenberg, Weinstein and Sweeny write, "The plain truth is that if we hire people whose motivation and abilities suit them to the position, then and only then can some of the external motivational approaches have a long-lasting, positive effect on productivity. Without the proper internal motivation, the externals can create motion but not consistent achievement."

To a large extent, motivational tools (compensation, bonuses, rewards, competitions, etc.) can serve as a very short-term incentive to bring attention to whatever metric you want to highlight at that point. They can occasionally create the illusion of performance from less stellar performers, and they sometimes reveal temporary false-positives that can, in the long term, create more harm than good. While we often lament results that show the same people winning sales contests time and again, the opposite affect would actually be much worse. Motivational tactics or strategies that are short lived, and which enable lesser performers to temporarily ascend the heady heights of your sales charts, may undermine those team members whose performance day in and day out consistently places them above their less accomplished colleagues, because they have the inherent wiring for the job and because they are already highly motivated to do the job.

In *Never Hire A Bad Salesperson Again*, Croner and Abraham write that "University of Memphis psychology professor Andrew Vinchur and his colleagues analyzed the results of 98 previous studies on personality factors that predict sales performance. These studies spanned the years from 1918 to 1996 and included a total of about 46,000 salespeople. Vinchur's group reported in 1998 that achievement motivation showed a stronger relationship to sales performance than any other trait." It is always possible to get someone to engage in activities or behaviors in the short term that they do not enjoy. That short-term focus and energy may even create a result that can convince a manager that things have changed. It is, by all accounts, an illusion. Unless the person is intrinsically motivated to do what it is they are being asked to do, they will do so only under duress (subtle or otherwise) and it will not last.

I'll leave the final word on the topic of motivation to Katherine Graham-Leviss, who writes in her book *The Perfect Hire*, "People are motivated to do what they want to do, not what you want them to do. So a lot of time gets wasted trying to manage your salespeople by attempting to motivate them, something that is quite impossible to do."

Where to Find
Salespeople

In my interactions with hiring managers I frequently hear that they just simply don't know where to find great salespeople. They will tell me that they have tried everything and that I just don't know "their market" and the challenges of finding great people.

I will repeat what I said earlier in this book: you need to look in different places for different things than you are looking for now. If you do that, you will realize that about 25% of the general population has the inherent wiring to become good salespeople but many of them are not working for your competitor or, in fact, in sales at all. Many of the people who might possibly have the wiring of a star sales performer have never given a minute's thought to the idea that they could have a very rewarding career in sales. They are employed, not all happily, in a myriad of occupations and careers and your job is to begin to peel back the layers of possibility to find them. Gallup's *State of the Workplace* report, conducted in 142 countries, found that only 13% of employees worldwide are truly engaged in their jobs. Even if we allow for some weighting on those statistics due to cultural, economic or other related matters in some of the countries studied, it is pretty clear that there are large numbers of people employed today in all of our communities who do not enjoy what they are doing. That presents great opportunities for active recruitment efforts, when combined with a structured hiring process.

Once you have established the criteria that you are looking for in a salesperson, it is important that you share it verbally and in writing. Tell your current employees, customers and contacts what you are looking for. Develop your own elevator pitch so that you can recite it at a moment's notice when you are out shopping yourself, when you are at the dentist's office, when you are at a restaurant, or when you are running errands. Being able to recite your elevator pitch will greatly enhance the likelihood of engaging people who will directly and indirectly respond to your message. Create your own little story and commit it to memory. It could be as simple as:

I'm looking for positive, high-energy people with a strong competitive spirit who are great listeners.

As simple as that single sentence is, it actually says a great deal. It says that you want competitive people. It says that you are looking for positive people with great energy. It says that you want someone who is a good listener. What it also says, by omission, is that you are not looking for people with experience. It opens that door wide for anyone that might be at all intrigued at the possibility of beginning a career in a sales environment. After you have developed your brief narrative, you need to begin to tell that story over and over at every opportunity.

I believe very strongly that your own network and your own employee base represent the best avenues for finding great new hires. Telling your story over and over will give your current contacts an opportunity to consider their friends, colleagues and their social network. I can already hear the chorus of readers agreeing with the above sentiment and wondering why you have just wasted your money buying this book when you were already tapping into your network. Here's why: you are likely hiring the wrong people from your current network. If your selection process for candidates that come through your immediate network (Friends and friends of friends, etc.) is as bad as it is for those candidates who come from outside your network—perhaps even worse (since there may be a false confidence because he or she is related to a current employee or customer) then you are probably hiring the wrong people for all the wrong reasons.

Yes, tap into your network as a great source of talent, but under no circumstances should you short-circuit the vetting or interview process because someone you know once went to school with someone you know or once worked with your sister. Let your contacts know that you would love to talk to anyone that they think might be a good fit but that you will put them through a stringent interview process before making any hiring decisions. If they are okay with that, bring them in for an interview and let the games begin.

The second thing to do is to place an advertisement in whatever digital or print vehicles that you think might work for you. There are so many places that an ad can be placed but the first thing to do is to get the copy right. The following example might be an interesting way to get the attention of people who do not have sales experience but who do posses the appropriate wiring:

Experience Not Wanted
Are You Ready For A Career Change?

If this is you, we want to talk to you:

- Upbeat, Positive and Energetic
- Good Listening and Communication Skills
- A Relationship Builder
- A Good Sense of Urgency
- Handle Setbacks in Stride
- Willing to Take a Risk
- Love to Work with Beautiful Products

If you are ready for a career change, or if you are considering reentering the workplace, we would like to talk to you.

Again, if we are looking to speak to people who have not already identified themselves as retail sales professionals, we must position the ad in a place where it will be seen by "non-sales people." I have had owners use ads similar to this and then render the approach useless by placing the ad in the sales section of Craigslist, or whatever site they select.

If you are trying to speak to people who do not currently work in sales then cast your line where those particular fish are swimming. Categories such as:

> **Customer Service**
> **Education**
> **Hospitality**
> **Marketing**
> **Fitness**
> **TV/Film/Video**

Your website should always reflect your desire to speak to quality talent. Put a brief narrative up that articulates the kind of person you are always interested in talking to, whether you are hiring or not. Your website is a fantastic communication vehicle about you and your company and it is a great place to connect with potential hires.

It is worth repeating that you should always be on the lookout for great talent. It will be a wonderful luxury if your pipeline is filled with great talent just waiting for the opportunity to come and work for you.

Any strategy that includes waiting to look for talent until you have an opening is doomed to failure. The added stress and anxiety of having to quickly fill a void is a recipe for quick and costly talent mistakes. At best, you may get a short-term fix (a warm body to cover immediate staffing needs) and a long-term headache.

Once upon a time all most businesses had to do to fill an open position was to advertise in the local newspaper and wait for the resumes to flood the mailbox. Those days are obviously long gone and the complexity of deciding where to advertise for talent has never been greater. That said, there are now myriad opportunities to connect quickly and succinctly with the right kind of candidates. Some of them are "old world" methods and some are more current. A partial list might include:

Suggestions for finding salespeople...

- ➤ **Your Website**
- ➤ **Employee referrals**
- ➤ **Networking**
- ➤ **Keeping your antennae up**
- ➤ **Simply Hired**
- ➤ **Glass Door.com**
- ➤ **AOL Find A Job**
- ➤ **Snag A Job.com**
- ➤ **USA Jobs**
- ➤ **Job.com**
- ➤ **Monster**
- ➤ **CareerBuilder**
- ➤ **Hot Jobs (www.hotjobs.yahoo.com)**
- ➤ **The Ladders (www.theladders.com)**
- ➤ **www.indeed.com**
- ➤ **www.simplyhired.com**
- ➤ **Craigslist**
- ➤ **Twitter**
- ➤ **Facebook**
- ➤ **Linkedin**
- ➤ **Recruiters**

12-Questions for Sales Candidates Without Experience

I f you have done your due diligence in exploring whether the resume is real and relevant—and whether the candidate might be a good fit for your culture—you can now turn to the questions that deal with sales wiring. As I have discussed throughout this book, you can get a great deal of the hiring process right, including culture and resume exploration, and still have the whole process of talent acquisition fall apart if the wiring is not there. At the risk of extreme and irritating redundancy, I am going to remind you that sales wiring cannot be taught, it cannot come as a consequence of a stellar compensation and/or reward system, and it certainly cannot be gleaned or assumed no matter how many years of mediocre performance (couched slightly differently by the candidate) your interviewee has.

Each question is open-ended and is designed to explore the three central elements of Drive, Empathy and Resilience. There are twelve questions in all and, while I am not suggesting that the questions must be asked in order, I have purposely laid them out in a way that makes each one unique so as to limit priming the candidate as to what they need to do to become an interview star. While one could make an argument that you could further juxtapose the resume and culture questions into these wiring questions (which must be added to the wiring questions), I would suggest handling each of the three distinct elements (resume, culture, wiring) separately.

The questions are designed to explore and, hopefully, uncover inherent wiring in candidates with little to no sales experience. These candidates would have been drawn to your advertisement, posting or networking and you want to understand what it was that drew them to your business and to uncover whether or not their wiring would suggest a good fit.

While all twelve of the questions are expressly designed for candidates without sales experience, many of them will also work for candidates with sales experience. Some others can work with very minor modifications. For instance *Tell Me How You Would Go About Building A Client Book?* for an inexperienced candidate becomes *Tell Me About Your Client Book* for an experienced candidate. *What Do You Think You Would Most Enjoy About Sales?* for an inexperienced candidate becomes *What Do You Enjoy Most About Sales?* for a candidate with experience.

Examples of questions that can work for both experienced and inexperienced candidates would include *What Are Your Favorite Activities Outside Of Work?* and *On A Scale Of 1-10, How Competitive Are You?*

I have included a few additional questions designed specifically for experienced candidates at the conclusions of the twelve questions. Those are questions that continue to drive at the inherent wiring (Drive, Empathy and Resilience). Let's start with the questions for candidates without sales experience.

What do you think you would most enjoy about sales?

This is one of the most direct, most relevant, and most telling of questions to ask a candidate. Whether you ask this question first or last is not that important, but it will go a long way towards helping you to understand the candidate's inherent wiring.

In reality, there is not a great deal of thought put into this very important question by people who have never been in sales. And, if we are being very honest, we might also acknowledge that few interviewers even seem to understand the significance of this question.

We ask this question so that we can get to the very heart of why the candidate is interviewing in the first place. The question might seem very obvious but it is rarely asked and rarely understood. There is a reason why more than half of the people currently employed in sales ought not to be. Somebody took the time and energy to interview each and every one of those people and felt like they had hired the best candidate under the circumstances. They were right about 42% of the time.

Each of those interviewers believed that they had appropriately communicated what the needs of the position were, and yet all too many of them suffered from what George Bernard Shaw described: "The single biggest problem in communication is the illusion that it has taken place."

Even for those of us who see the need to sell, to persuade, to influence, and to really own the relationship, as an obvious function of the salesperson's job, we still believe somehow that we are on the same page as the applicant. We rationalize they must surely understand those fundamental tenets, when we are, in fact, very often miles apart.

The candidate may subconsciously believe that the job of the salesperson has very little to do with actually selling. They may be of the opinion that when a customer wants something he or she will simply point to it and tell you that they want it. They may believe that their job is to educate themselves on a laundry list of features and benefits, so that they can deliver them in a perfectly rehearsed presentation to each customer, whether that customer wants that or not.

That product-focused attitude is how most salespeople approach their jobs and the customer, whose shopping experiences vacillate between information dump and absolute indifference, has such low expectations that they don't even expect to be heard or understood. Therein, of course, is a huge opportunity for those sales professionals and stores that really place an emphasis on hiring the very best people for the job.

What we really need to sense from the candidate in response to this question is an intuitive awareness of what the sales process actually entails, and why that candidate believes that, despite their lack of experience, he or she would likely be successful in a sales role. We are not looking to hear time-worn clichés such as "I like people," or "I love what you sell!" Of course those things are important. In fact, they are very important. They do not, however, give us the real information that we need.

It is much easier to find someone who likes people, and who will enjoy working with your wonderful merchandise, than it is to find both of those attributes wrapped in a salesperson with the ability and drive to actually sell something.

There are numerous good answers to the question provided it speaks to the candidate's competitiveness, their love of winning, their need to persuade, their appetite for a challenge, etc.

Great salespeople love to help their customers find solutions. They see their role as taking charge of the situation and working with the customer to ensure a successful conclusion to the customer's needs.

When I asked a friend of mine, and a great salesperson, Hae Yon Bigby, what she most enjoyed about sales, she said, "Knowing that I can help them find what they are looking for. I like the hunt."

We want to hear answers that get to the heart of great sales wiring. A candidate who talks about her desire to persuade, of her great listening skills and her ability to stay focused in the face of rejection, of her sense of urgency, her love of winning, of seeing her name on the top of the scorecard, is more likely to be successful in a sales.

Somewhere within their experiences in previous jobs, social calendars and interests, school experiences, etc., there is a very clear indication as to whether that drive and that wiring is there. Your job is to uncover those traits.

There are many good answers that appropriately speak to this kind of wiring. If you do not hear a response that touches on the aforementioned, go back to the question later on in the interview and unapologetically ask it again. Tell the applicant that it is important that you understand their motivation for interviewing for a sales position. Restate the question and remain quiet while the candidate attempts to answer it again.

One of the great danger zones for interviewers, especially those folks who do not interview for a living (and even some of those who do) is that we can sometimes, without even knowing we are doing it, answer the question for the candidate. Think about it. How many times have you heard something like this:

"What do you like most about the sales job? I mean, do you like meeting new people or is it about the lovely merchandise or..."

Ask the question in a direct and concise fashion and stop talking. If you are asked for clarity, go ahead and clarify as best you can, but do not answer the question for the candidate and please, please learn to embrace silence after you have asked your question. If you ask *and* answer the question, you will have paved the way for an intuitive candidate to see the roadmap and self-servingly navigate through the interview. What you may well get, as a consequence of asking and answering your own questions (it happens more than you can imagine), is the appearance of a great candidate, and a great fit—and what you will have bought is a command performance by someone whose best work was the interview itself.

Asking direct questions is not designed to make the candidate uneasy or to trip them up. If you have done your job well, you should have made the applicant feel comfortable and you are now simply exploring whether this situation can be a win-win for your company and for the applicant. Remember, there is no such thing as a win-lose or a lose-win. If your employee likes working for your company but your company is less than thrilled with his or her sales productivity that is not a good situation. Conversely, if you really like your employee but he or she is not happy in their work, that too will be a problem that will likely end in a premature separation.

Being direct and honest with the candidate is the very best thing you can do for them. It clearly establishes what your priorities are and it provides the applicant with the opportunity to conclude whether the fit is right for them or not.

In the event that you are interviewing a candidate with sales experience, the question can be tweaked to ask them, *"What do you most enjoy about sales?"* If he or she has spent some number of years in a sales environment, and the wiring is not there, it never will be, no matter how many years of experience they acquire.

In interviewing candidates with sales experience, you need to ensure that you don't let the facts gets in the way of the truth. What I mean by that is that your candidate may tell you that she was the number one sales producer in her previous job. Her personal sales may well have exceeded X or Y, but if she was the best salesperson on a very weak sales team, that would be a good example of a fact not being the same as a truth and a hiring decision based on that fact could haunt you for years as you patiently wait to see her great sales wiring emerge.

Asking the candidate to tell you why she was the best salesperson in her previous job, and asking her to give you specific examples of why she believed she was the most effective sales producer, can reveal an entirely different picture than what the facts alone suggest.

Once you have identified the facts, you can begin the process of uncovering the truth. Was she the best performer on a very bad team? Was she a "top performer" despite a wiring ill-suited to sales? Did she cost the company money by discounting her way to gross sales results? What was the context of the sales results? Did she clerk a product that requires little sales expertise?

Again, it is so important that we uncover the wiring of the candidate. The facts can help us get there, but they should never be taken at face value without deeper conversation and clarification of context.

Describe a situation when an idea of yours was rejected and tell me how you felt about that...

We are really trying to understand two very important and fundamental questions here. In the first instance, it is imperative that anyone who is going to make their living in sales understands that frequent rejection is part and parcel of the job. The second important question that we are seeking to understand is whether the candidate has the innate capacity to tell relevant stories.

We are not looking to feed the old myth of salespeople talking customers into submission. Talkers exist, no doubt. They are oftentimes the very people who impress us as great sales candidates because of their seemingly endless capacity to talk. It is not about talking; it is about engaging in a way that is relevant to the customer or, in this instance, the interviewer. To that extent, we want to know whether the candidate has really understood the question (empathy), whether he can connect it to a relevant experience in his life or career, and how he appears to have coped with the rejection (resilience) he used as an example.

A candidate who is incapable of tapping into his own stories and experiences—when he has the carrot of winning an important job by doing so—will not likely fare any better in a retail environment where storytelling is an essential characteristic of the job. If, on the other hand, we find that the candidate easily taps into his memory bank—and can relate relevant and interesting examples of having made suggestions, tried new things, pushed the envelope in work, in academia, in life—it portends well for that candidate in a sales environment. It suggests that there could well be sufficient reserves of empathy, storytelling and resilience to handle the daily setbacks and frequent rejections.

It is a mathematical certainty that even the very best retail salespeople will be rejected more often than they will make a sale. Whether her conversion rate is 20%, 30%, or even a potentially very impressive, 40%, somewhere between six out of ten and eight out of ten people are very likely walking out of your stores empty-handed. Suffice to say, any salesperson that does not possess the capacity to deal with rejection on a daily basis will not perform at a high level.

To be clear, we are not looking for people who welcome rejection, or who like it any more than the next person. What I am saying, however, is that great salespeople have the ability to keep rejection in perspective. They understand that it is a necessary evil and they do not allow the disappointment of a missed sale from deterring them from their next opportunity. Even if you train and retrain a person to ask for the sale as an essential requirement of your work environment, you can be certain that her willingness to continue to do so will ultimately be consumed by her inability to deal with the constant rejection that is a given in all retail stores.

Once again, great salespeople do not like rejection any more than poor salespeople. They do not, however, allow the rejection to define who they are and, most importantly, they never let it dampen their enthusiasm for the next prospect or the next opportunity. Buckingham and Coffman write in *First Break All The Rules*, "By studying the best salespeople, great sales managers have learned that the best, just like the worst, suffer call reluctance. Apparently, the best salesperson, as with the worst, feels as if he is selling himself. It is this striving talent of feeling personally invested in the sale that causes him to be so persuasive but it also causes him to take rejection personally—every time he makes a sales call he feels the shiver of fear that someone will say no to him, to *him*. The difference between greatness and failure in sales is that the great salesperson is not paralyzed by this fear."

Like most everything else, I am certain that there are numerous websites, classes, books and trained professionals out there somewhere that purport to improve a person's resilience. And, without casting aspersions on any opinion to the contrary, I am saying, without reservation, that if you hire people who allow themselves to be defined by rejection, if you hire people who cringe every time they hear someone say *no*, if you hire people who avoid asking tough questions, so as to protect themselves from rejection, you will not turn that person into a great sales producer, no matter what training, therapy, literature, or compensation you throw at them.

Ask the question and listen very closely to the answer. If the candidate does not seem to understand what you are asking, restate the question. Listen for what the candidate is saying and also observe her body language as she responds. Is the response relevant? Is the body language consistent with what you are hearing? In other words, are you hearing her talk about how she was a little disappointed by a particular rejection, while her body language seems to collapse under the emotional weight of her recall of that rejection? Be prepared to ask a follow-up question such as "What did you learn from that experience?" Was it, in fact, a learning experience or does the response suggest that the rejection elicited an element of trauma that might be revealing and, potentially, damaging in a high-rejection environment such as sales?

In response to this question, we want to hear very specific, very relevant examples of rejection that show the candidate as having the strength to overcome disappointments and the perseverance and resilience to not be defined by those failures.

What are your favorite activities outside of work?

We reveal a great deal about ourselves in everything we choose to do with our free time. Most of us have great passions for hobbies, or activities and understanding the drivers behind those choices can offer a wonderful insight into the kind of people we are.

For instance, if a candidate responds to this question by telling you that she loves to curl up on a couch in a quiet room and lose herself in a great book that can be a good thing or it might not be such a good thing. On the one hand, it might signal that she is the kind of person who loves to expand her horizons through continued learning. It might suggest that she aspires to maintain a nice balance in her life with a combination of active and sedentary interests. It could be that she is so active, so driven, that she needs to recharge her batteries by "switching off" for a bit with a great book.

Conversely, it might also signal that she is not exactly cut out for the hustle and bustle of a high-pressure sales floor and the demands of retail in general. Exploring the interests and passions of a candidate can enable the interviewer to better understand the inherent wiring of that person so that you can determine if a sedentary interest is about recharging otherwise hard-driven batteries, or a need to escape a job that is at odds with that person's real wiring. If it is the former, then it ought not to be a concern. If, on the other hand, it is the latter, you must further explore why immersion into the high-pressure, high-performance theater of retail makes sense for you or for the candidate.

My wife has a friend who regularly talks about wanting to learn more about her particular profession. She espouses great envy at those people around her who seem to have a better handle on their work and on the many facets and complexities that it can throw at them on a given day. However, when my wife suggests particular reading material—books, blogs, industry magazines, etc.—her friend responds that she doesn't have time to read. That is what I call a whale of a disconnect. If the will and, more importantly, the wiring are there, people make time for the things that are important to them. If, like most of us, the candidate leads a particularly busy life, she will be even more selective about those things that she elects to pursue during her limited free time and that prioritization can be very telling.

I happen to be a voracious reader of books, balancing my choices between business, psychology, mysteries, memoirs, biographies, etc. In short, I am always looking to expand my knowledge on subjects of interest to me and reading, writing or discussing those subjects is as much a part of who I am and what I do as enjoying my kids' baseball and soccer games, enjoying a night out with my wife, or listening to a great Frank Sinatra album. In many respects, our interests and passions are a calling of sorts. They seem to select us as much as we select them and they reveal a great deal about us.

There are, I suspect, precious few people, who proclaim to want to learn more, and to materially increase their base of knowledge and understanding in their desired discipline, who have no time at all to pursue it. It is, for want of a better expression, hard-wired. If the will and the wiring are inherent, embrace of the tasks, topics, learning and activities will come very naturally.

As a recent Gallup study suggests, only 30% of employees in the United States are engaged in their jobs. 52% are not engaged and 18% are actively disengaged. With those numbers we can safely assume that we can actually learn more about a person by exploring their interests than we can by examining their employment history. Another statistical probability, given the Gallup study, is that we probably have some of those disengaged employees within our own companies and amongst the candidates we will be interviewing.

By asking the candidate to talk about her interests and passions, we are giving her a safe platform to discuss her own wiring. What we ideally want to hear is that she engages in activities that further her learning, or which suggest a drive or competitiveness, or which put her in and around people in social situations. Activities that are inherently challenging, such as playing or coaching sports, playing an instrument in a band, singing in a choir, organizing fundraisers, teaching a class at a local college, etc., could reveal a person with ambition and a desire to connect with people.

If she is organizing social groups, constantly networking and driven by the opportunity to be with and around people all the time, the signs point to someone with the demeanor to be very comfortable in the madness of a hectic retail environment. I have yet to meet a great salesperson who is not turbo-charged during the busiest times at the prospect of engaging with more customers and closing more sales. We should be looking for signs of that in their chosen interests.

If she says that there is no place in the world she would rather be than on that couch, in that quiet room, at every available opportunity, I would argue that this is probably not someone who thrives in, and craves, the action typical of an energized retail environment. She may be overwhelmed by the hustle and bustle of a busy retail store and she may, quietly and subconsciously, seek refuge at the very times when you need her most. Again, few single answers give us all of the information we need, but we cannot afford to ignore major disconnects.

When I asked some great salespeople what they were passionate about, one of them, Teri Ramirez, talked about her volunteer work with Delta Theta Chi, a National Women's Sorority that helps foster children acclimate into the real world after they turn 18, and are lost to the system.

Rich Pesqueira spoke about his devotion to his wife, his love of music, karate and scuba-diving. Hae Yon Bigby talked about her family and—though she did not mention it in our interview—I know that she too is a compulsive and observant shopper. Dave Padget talked about his wife of thirty-three years and his passion for college basketball, college football and major golf events.

Ann DeMarias and Valerie White write in *First Impressions*, "Talking about parts of your life about which you feel passionate, whether it is work, an interest in running, or watching horror films, generally sends very positive messages. That's because when you talk about what excites you, it's like reliving your experience. Your body language—gesturing, smiling, and laughing—is appealing and infectious."

Another interesting tidbit that my friend, and superstar salesperson, Teri Ramirez shared, was that she loves to shop. "I am very, very passionate about shopping. It puts me in a zone. I shop every week, for clothes, for shoes, for antiques and books and collectables. I shop in big stores, little stores, mall stores, estate sales. I am always looking to see what I can learn and from whom." Teri, like many great salespeople, is wired for the job that she does—and she does it at a very high level of performance. There is no switch that goes on when she enters her place of employment, any more than there is a switch goes off when she leaves it. Those two areas, work and outside interests, are essentially intertwined and her actions and activities in one begets and connects with the actions and activities in the other.

Great salespeople crave action. They are never more relaxed than when they are, as Teri said, "in the zone." Like Teri, they rarely switch off because they are wired to move, to engage, to learn, to connect.

Another good reason to ask a candidate about her interests outside of work is that those hobbies and activities that mean a great deal to us are as much a part of our lives as other aspects of it, including work. As Levin and Rosse write in *Talent Flow*, "An employee who places a lot of value on a hobby or other interest may be motivated to remain with a particular employer who accommodates that interest." There could, of course, be a downside to the hobby or interest if it threatens to interfere with the job requirements, something that you would want to know in advance of making the hire.

Why do you think I should hire someone with no sales experience?

This is a very direct way of asking the candidate to sell himself to you. There was obviously something in your job posting that spoke to him and you need to understand what that is and how relevant that might be for your needs.

It is conceivable that what brought him in was the idea that he just didn't have to have any sales experience. In his mind, there might be some kind of warped logic that has him all excited about the "no experience required" part and, as he was never too keen on the idea of a sales career to begin with (yes, people do take jobs all the time that they are neither wired for, nor particularly interested in) why not apply for it!

When push comes to shove, there are lots of people who take jobs that they are neither qualified for nor particularly interested in for the long haul. As mentioned earlier, a cursory glance at some of the studies available on the topic of employee engagement will show that as many as 80% of employees are not engaged in their work. Those people all went through an interview process and convinced a hiring manager that they were the right choice. Of course, there may be reasons other than wiring that have the employee disengaged—poor management is often cited as a reason why people want to leave their jobs—but some significant number of those people are simply not wired to do the job they were hired to perform and that uncomfortable fit ultimately catches up to them.

Your candidate may have responded simply because he needs a job, or because he hates the job he has, and your posting might have struck him as the very best "temporary" situation he could pursue right now. He may be of the opinion that a few good heaves of hope against any willing wall will find him a paycheck and provide his next stepping stone on the road to no place in particular. It may also have occurred to him that your ad and he might actually be a marriage made in Heaven, since you requested what he doesn't have (experience) and you are offering an opportunity to do something that he has little interest in doing (sales), but which clearly can't be that hard if you don't need any experience to do it.

He may, on the other hand, have responded to the posting because it touched a nerve with him and because he is intrigued by what he read in the advertisement. He might be excited by the possibilities of what your needs are and how they could relate to him. The language you used in your posting may have intrigued him to the point that he recognized himself in the posting. He may, in fact, be exactly what you are looking for, someone with the essential wiring to become great in sales, but who may not yet have discovered those qualities in himself in a professional sales environment.

What you want to hear in response to this question is how and why the job posting spoke to him. You want to be persuaded by his drive and sincerity, and by his commitment to working in and understanding a sales environment and its myriad demands. Ideally, you want to see a passion for people, real enthusiasm about the possibility of starting a career in sales and great excitement about working in your store. At a minimum, what you must hear is that some specific language in the job posting aligned with his sense of his own strengths and interests.

For instance, he may say that your posting spoke to the need for the candidate to have a competitive drive and, while he may never have worked in sales previously, he recognizes a competitive drive in himself. He should be able to support that with a brief narrative from a previous job, from his academic career, or from his interests and activities outside of work. He may say that your posting requested a candidate with good listening skills or with strong resilience, and he may be able to support that with a story or two demonstrating his great listening skills, or his capacity for overcoming failure, disappointment and rejection.

If he is able to articulate, in a believable and persuasive way (don't fall for the latter without the former), that the language in the job posting spoke directly to him, and that he is genuinely intrigued and excited about the possibility of exploring a new career direction, then you are off to a great start.

If the best the candidate can offer is that the posting said that he didn't need to have experience, and, he has, as it happens, no experience, that is not a good sign and your antennae ought to be raised very high. Again, remember that you are trying to hire someone who can persuade with sincerity. If he cannot sell you on himself at this early stage of the interview, you are probably talking to the wrong candidate.

Tell me about a failure of yours...

This is another way to revisit the idea of resilience, storytelling and, in some respects, the candidate's honesty. We have all had failures in our careers and it is not unreasonable to expect that we have learned a few things from them. In telling those stories, we have the opportunity to establish a level of competence in verbal communication and, in tapping into our own reservoir of experiences, we have the opportunity to demonstrate how honest and open we are about our own failures.

There are many things that we can put on our resumes, but what we all have in common, is that we will always frame our experiences in the very best light. Few of us will ever list our failures on our resumes. No one would expect it of us. It is human nature to expect that we will attempt to suppress our bad experiences and, absent a compelling reason to do otherwise, not want to talk about them.

To be fair, we, as potential hiring managers, might never have agreed to the interview in the first place if the candidate had indicated that he left a particular job because he couldn't get along with his boss. We wouldn't likely proceed further if a resume indicated that an applicant went months, perhaps even years, without meeting his sales goals.

We are unlikely to read about his chronically bad punctuality during a period where he had pressing personal issues, or how an important project was negatively impacted by his lack of preparedness.

Every single one of us has a laundry list of things that we are not overly proud of. Whether it takes us back to school, to previous employment, or even to failures in our personal lives, we all have the list and we ought to be able to tap into it and tell a story or two about ourselves and how we overcame our failures.

This is not the forum to listen to stories of failed romantic relationships, or other matters so personal as to create an uncomfortable situation for the interviewer or the interviewee. A candidate who has empathy and resilience (and we do not want them for sales if they lack either of these essential characteristics) should be able to tap into his experiences and share with you some of his failures and tell you what he has learned from those experiences.

I once made a judgment call about a candidate that cost my employer unnecessary financial losses and which came back to haunt me. I had interviewed a man for a loss-prevention position. This position had as much to do with customer service (directing customers to different areas of the store when asked) as it had with security, nonetheless there was a significant enough component that exposed the company to risk. The loss prevention officers were, on occasion, required to be alone with products as they were transported from the sales floor to the vault at the end of the business day.

The candidate's resume and his background (and I should point out that there was no evidence of previous criminal activity) did not quite suggest that this guy was the best candidate for the job. There was really nothing in his background that indicated that he had been previously entrusted with the responsibility for sensitive merchandise. In short, I had allowed myself to be won over by his personal story and, while I was intuitive enough to know that I was taking a calculated risk, I was also committed to being the guy that helped get this fellow on a path to respectability by giving him the break his career had previously lacked.

In truth, I saw what I wanted to see and I suspect that I became consumed, to the point of blindness, in the idea that I was going to be the knight in shining armor for this guy's career. I married my own biases early on in the interview and I probably missed all kinds of telltale signs that could have served as a warning, if I had been open to them.

With the benefit of hindsight, I know that further due diligence might have shown the candidate to have been too great a risk for the position in question and yet I failed to peel back the layers of that particular onion to my company's detriment. My biases created a risk for my employer that resulted in unnecessary losses.

I can still recall sitting in court, as we attempted to prosecute the man for the theft of some jewelry items, and lamenting my poor judgment, even as I still found myself subconsciously rooting for him to use this experience to propel himself to better things in his life.

I can talk about that failure now and say, without a shadow of doubt, that it serves as a reminder to me that I cannot and must not allow my own agenda (the chivalrous knight on a white horse) to govern my choices. It was my failure and it stands to this day as a great education for me.

Your candidate must be honest enough to select an example or two of past failures and humble enough to articulate where they went wrong and what they have learned from those past failures. The example I used was from a professional experience but the principle works equally well even if you are interviewing a candidate who is fresh from school, without previous work history.

Be warned, if you ask the candidate to tell you about a failure of theirs and what they have learned from it, any version of "In my desire to get the job done well, I can be impatient with my colleagues," run, don't walk, to the nearest exit. That response, and its near and distant cousins, is one of the most meaningless, one of the most tired responses to this or related questions and ought to be called out as such.

This is neither the time nor place for principled posturing from the candidate. You want to hear very specific examples of a very real failure and a very clear articulation of what lessons were learned from it.

When you are shopping, what kind of salesperson impresses you?

It is often said that it is virtually impossible to be objective about one-self. To that extent, by asking the candidate to describe the qualities that she most associates with good salespeople when she is shopping we are giving her a very safe platform (it is about someone else, not me) to articulate the kind of salesperson that she herself may become, or may aspire to.

In identifying what she likes as a shopper, if she describes characteristics that are very service oriented ("I don't like being approached right away" or "I want to be left alone when I am shopping" or "I don't like pushy salespeople," etc.) she may well be constructing the roadmap for the kind of salesperson she will become if you were to hire her. It is hard to imagine that anyone who would extol the virtues of being *left alone* in a retail store will be comfortable engaging customers the way that great salespeople are driven to do on a daily basis.

If, however, she describes a salesperson who respects her time, and who takes charge and delivers a solution to her needs, you are likely seeing a candidate who views the role of a salesperson as solution-based—and who sees her job as owning the responsibility to make the sale and to make the customer happy.

A salesperson who fundamentally understands and recognizes that the customer comes into your store for a reason, and who enjoys actually selling something, is going to be infinitely more successful in delivering results and building rewarding and sustained relationships for the store and for your customers.

This is a good place to delve a little deeper by asking the candidate to describe a couple of experiences from her own shopping experiences that demonstrate what she liked and did not like. People generally love to tell stories (if your candidate does not, it ought to be a caution) and it is our job to glean the relevant information from those stories.

Pay attention to both the style and the substance when listening to her stories. Does she sound interesting? Does she have an engaging personality and do you find yourself getting drawn into her stories? Are her stories on message or do they ramble all over the place to the point of distraction? Is she putting you to sleep? Most importantly, what message or messages are you getting from her stories that indicate the kind of salesperson she might become and how do those stories inform and invigorate the interview process?

A well-presented story that is interesting and focused, and which speaks to characteristics that are relevant to the sales process, can be a very powerful tool in understanding the candidate's inherent wiring. As we listen to the stories being told, we are hearing that candidate's idea of what a good salesperson looks and sounds like.

In Guber's *Tell To Win* he writes, "Whatever story you tell, if you are perceived to be authentic, your audience will hear you empathetically and be more likely to embrace your passion." That sounds like a pretty good recipe for what a great salesperson ought to sound like.

It is almost unimaginable that two great lessons on what "permission to buy" means were delivered in the same store, with the same item of furniture, by four different salespeople, years apart—but that is exactly what happened to me.

For reasons I still don't fully understand, I visited the furniture department of my local department store one Saturday afternoon with my two then-young sons. As we strolled through the store, a couch caught my eye and I immediately fell in love with it. I didn't go into that store looking for a couch and I certainly didn't need a couch, but that had nothing whatsoever to do with anything. I simply loved it.

As I stood there, admiring my newfound love, my two boys were getting a little restless, feeling decidedly less enamored by the couch than their dad. After a few minutes, a salesperson approached me from behind and asked...wait for it, "Can I help you?" Before I could tell her how terribly hard I had fallen for this magnificent work of art—err, couch—I replied, "I'm just looking, thanks!" and off she wandered, back from whence she had come, presumably muttering to herself that I was just a time-waster, and satisfied that she had done her bit for the cause.

A minute or two later, I succumbed to the pleadings of my sons and we ambled off to the local Lids store to add to their growing collection of baseball hats. A couple of weeks later, again with my reluctant sons in tow, I revisited my beloved couch and almost the exact same scene played out. A different salesperson approached me this time and asked the same tired question and, surprise, surprise, she responded the same way when I sprayed myself with the "just-looking" repellant. As if following a company mandate, she too turned on her heels and left me and the boys with the couch. A few moments later, we too turned and left the couch, and the assortment of disengaged and uninterested salespeople, behind.

I saw no oddity in having gone to visit my beloved couch again, even as I waited for some divine intervention to persuade me to buy it. After all, I loved it. It wasn't a question of need, it quite simply spoke to me in a way that I could not easily understand but the collective indifference of the store's salespeople managed to keep us separated.

A couple of weeks later I returned to visit the couch again, expecting it to have a "sold" sign on it, or for it to be gone altogether. Alas, that bad boy was still present and, as I stood there ruminating on our as-yet unconsummated relationship, a confident voice from behind said, "She's a beauty isn't she? Why don't you take a seat and see how she feels?" For the first time in three visits, I had been emotionally engaged and, surprise, surprise, I bought the couch that day.

As I mentioned, I didn't need a couch. In fact, buying it presented me with a minor dilemma, as I had nowhere to put it, given that I already owned a perfectly good couch. That said, I had, for the first time in three visits, been given permission to buy. That salesman assumed the sale and he addressed me as though my owning that couch was the most obvious and logical thing in the world.

I must assume that those three salespeople were on commission and that they each had sales targets to meet, and yet the first two salespeople expected the very least of me. They approached me as if just that exercise in and of itself allowed them to check some imaginary box ("I've done my job!") which then allowed them to return to whatever conversation they were having at the back of the store with their colleagues.

I also imagined, after their colleague had given me "permission to buy" the couch and had processed the sale, they complained about how *lucky* he was. How he always seemed to just walk into sales, while they had to work so hard to make a sale by dealing with all the tire-kickers. By assuming the sale, and believing the very best of the customer, the successful salesperson had given me permission to buy that couch. I was almost relieved when he assumed ownership as I was probably on my last visit before passing it up completely. In truth, I had given that store what very few prospects will give a store: multiple chances to get it right. They had not earned that right but, thanks to my persistence, and the competence of the third salesperson who approached me, I had given them the sale. For those of you keeping score, you are probably wondering where the fourth salesperson comes into this story?

To wit, some years later, my wife and I walked into the very same store and, strolling through the furniture department, we happened upon, yes, you guessed it, a couch that we both loved. Actually, it was a sectional, but we really did like it. We had not considered ourselves to be "sectional people" but this spoke to us in all the right ways and we really liked it. Heck, we even went as far as to sit in it. We liked the color, we liked how it felt when we sat in it, we liked its styling and, most of all, we believed it would work wonderfully well in our family room. We left the store that night and we did not buy that sectional.

While we were sitting there, a salesperson walked over and asked (you couldn't make this stuff up!), "Can I help you?" We engaged with her for a minute or two and then she strolled away, seemingly called to wherever that place is that calls when a salesperson does that mysterious shuffling retreat. She had not asked us for the sale. She never gave us "permission to buy." She obviously assumed that if we wanted the sectional we would have told her. We might even have pointed to it and with happily nodding heads produced our credit card. We did none of those things and she never made the sale.

Later that night I asked my wife if she would have bought the sectional if the salesperson had asked for the sale and she said yes. I felt exactly the same way, but we didn't buy it then, and we have not gone back to the store since. All the salesperson had to do was to assume the sale, engage us in a conversation about delivery times or methods of payment and she would have had our business.

Three out of four salespeople in that very same store all expected the least of us and they were rewarded with a self-fulfilling prophecy. How many times a day do you think that happens in that store? How many sales are lost? How many customers, like my wife and I, were denied the opportunity to make a purchase because a salesperson expected the least of us?

On a scale of 1–10, how competitive are you?

This is one of the very best questions you can ask someone who aspires to become a salesperson. Whether the candidate answers with a low number, a high number, or a number somewhere in between, the response will provide a great forum for discussion and further exploration. For instance, if she tells you that she would give herself a three or four, what you might be hearing is someone who does not view sales as a competitive environment and does not view herself as a competitive person. That's a problem. Her view of the sales world might be that it is a good place for pleasant personalities, good people skills, and for folks who like to get along. She would of course be mostly right in all of the aforementioned. We would be just fine if our salespeople had pleasant personalities, great people skills and a respectful sense of what it is like to be a part of a team. Those qualities, however, absent the drive to compete, will not deliver a salesperson who is a real difference-maker in a performance environment. If she scores herself low, follow up by asking her directly why she thinks someone who is not competitive would do well in a sales environment.

Your job is to understand if her inherent wiring is a good fit for sales and this is as good a place as any to learn some really valuable insights about the candidate. Ask her to describe some situations (sports are always good, musical competitions, auditions for plays, etc.) where she had to be competitive and try to glean whether her self-score aligns with her experiences and the accompanying narrative. If her stories reflect a general ambivalence in competitive arenas, you should credit her with knowing herself very well, acknowledge her honesty, but do not give her a job in sales.

If the candidate answers that she is a five or a six, you should delve into that by asking her why she rates herself at or slightly above the midpoint. It may be that she doesn't want to come across as arrogant or overly confident (even though great sales producers rarely worry about such matters) or it may be that she is actually being very honest and she is just not that competitive. A little humility is not necessarily a bad thing if it is married to a competitive drive. If however, her self-score reflects someone who has generally been at the middle of the pack in competitive endeavors—and who may be very comfortable with that—you are probably not looking at a potential star salesperson. Again, I would acknowledge her honesty and her sense of self, but I would not hire her for a sales job—unless you are anxious to build a team of mid-level performers.

If she answers the question by giving herself a nine or a ten, you have a great opportunity to explore the reasons for that self-score. In the best scenario, she gave herself that score because it accurately reflected her sense of self. We then want to hear that her stories and her narrative support that assessment. She may tell you about sporting accomplishments, academic accomplishments or previous wins (sales or otherwise) in her background. You want her to give you specific examples of why a high self-score is accurate and you need to decide whether that is a true reflection of her drive or whether it is false bravado—a result of her desire to impress you and to win the job.

I was once interviewing a candidate in Miami and I asked the candidate to rate himself from 1–10. The candidate's response was that he was a 10½ out of 10. While I admired his confidence and his desire to communicate his competitive spirit, his answer was completely at odds with what we had learned about him in our conversation up to that point.

What he had communicated so beautifully was his love for his children, his great sense of responsibility to them, his respect for his father and his dismay over the decline of his father's building supply business. These were all very admirable qualities and he was very successful in selling me and the other interviewers on his qualities as a first-rate human being, a father, a good son and provider for his family. We loved him and we were, naturally, won over by his inherent decency and goodness.

What he did not communicate, however, was that he was competitive. His answers to many of our questions did not suggest a wiring that was right for sales. He did not convince us that he could be persuasive enough in a sales environment and he most certainly did not justify giving himself a score of 10½ out of 10. It was well intentioned but, ultimately, false bravado. It came from the right place, his desire to please and his confidence in himself, but it did not reflect his inherent wiring.

One of the real giveaways for me was when I asked him what else he was doing to find suitable employment. He so casually responded that he had submitted applications to the Home Depot and to Lowes, that I suspected he had not tried very hard to secure employment with either of those two retailers. Given that he would seem to have been a perfect fit, very sincere, hardworking, a good knowledge of many of the products that those retailers sold, I was both surprised and disappointed to learn that he had not been more assertive in selling himself to those two companies.

What I wanted to hear was that he was showing up once a week to say hello to the managers or assistant managers to let them know that he was out there and just chomping at the bit to work for them. I wanted to hear that he was respectfully making a nuisance of himself by continually touching base to find out when (not if) they were going to hire him. He was not, of course, doing any of that. He had gone through the motions of submitting his applications and he was content to letting the process unfold, or not, without any attempt to influence decision makers in either of those two companies. Any suggestion that he was going to be more effective selling luxury products than he had been selling himself to Lowes or to the Home Depot would, I'm afraid, not have been very believable.

This young man had put on his best suit, perhaps his only suit. He was invested enough in the possibility of being hired that he showed up early for the interview. He was sincere and likeable throughout the interview and he was respectful and thoughtful in answering all of the questions that we put to him. He was exactly the kind of candidate that my clients had hired previously (albeit with a good deal more emphasis on jewelry experience) because, like most of us, they were drawn to good and decent people. If you are in any way sympathetic, it is so easy to fall in love with a candidate like this and to believe that his inherent decency and work ethic will ultimately overcome any obstacles that might come his way.

Asking him to rate himself on a scale of 1–10 enabled us to put into perspective his many good qualities and to understand better his lack of sales wiring. We were able to compare his self-rating with the stories he had told us to see if there was alignment or misalignment in his narrative. Unfortunately for the candidate, and fortunately for the business, we were able to see that there was complete misalignment between how he had graded himself and what he had been telling us. Despite giving himself a score of 10 ½ out of 10, this young man's narrative suggested that he was not very competitive and that he lacked the assertiveness necessary to be successful in a sales environment. He possessed many good and admirable qualities but drive was not principle amongst them.

To the eternal credit of my client, she later called the Home Depot on his behalf to recommend him for a position. I don't know whether they ever followed up with him or not to conduct a formal interview, but I suspect he would make a great hire in a service-driven business.

Very directly, asking the candidate why he or she gave themselves the score they did can be very revealing. If the candidate answers 10, an obvious follow-up question is to ask them why they rate themselves a 10. Questions such as "Tell me why you would rate yourself a 10?" and "Give me a couple of examples of your competitiveness" are good responses to that kind of self-score and will help us reconcile the self-assessment with reality.

During that same interview session in Miami, we interviewed another candidate who answered by saying that she would rate herself a 10 on the competitive scale. Her score was completely consistent with the narrative that accompanied her responses throughout the interview. We followed up the self-assessment by asking her why she gave herself a 10 and she was able to give us some very good examples from her previous work experience to support that score.

As it transpired, her background had been in collections, not sales, and yet she seemed to have the perfect wiring for the position. She demonstrated a strong competitive desire by giving us very specific examples and she also revealed great empathy in telling us stories of her interactions in the very competitive and challenging world of collections. She was hired for the position despite having no direct experience in sales and she has started out very strongly in her new career path.

The same question asked of two separate candidates, on the same day as it happens, revealed (more or less) the same self-score. The stories that each of the two candidates told to support their respective scores uncovered an entirely different narrative and reality. It showed that one candidate had a much stronger likelihood of succeeding in sales and the other did not have the wiring to be successful in a competitive sales environment.

What aspect of sales do you think would be most challenging for you?

In interviewing candidates who have no sales experience it is very important to understand whether they have given the world of sales any real thought at all in advance of the interview. If they have not done so, you should prepare for a short interview and explore other candidates. If they have, on the other hand, given a good deal of thought to what the world of sales might be like, you want to explore their perceptions to see if they align with what you are looking for.

As with all of these questions, there are multiple answers to this question and any one of them can lead you into a great conversation on the topic. For instance, if, as I heard recently, a candidate expresses concerns about working on Saturdays or on evenings, you are likely heading down the wrong path by reassuring them that the hours are really not that bad. Retail hours generally require a commitment to one if not both weekend days and almost always have some component of evening requirements.

This is the reality of the retail experience and, accepting that we want our lines in the water when the fish are swimming, there is rarely a scenario when we would not want our best people working during our busiest times. If there are concerns from the candidate about the requirement to work retail hours before they even start in the position, that concern will likely get worse after you have made the hire.

If you hear from the candidate that she worries about being too pushy, or about having to assert herself as a salesperson, that too ought to be a major red flag and should be explored before proceeding further. What you may be hearing in the first instance is someone who is perfectly willing to accept a sales position as long as it doesn't interfere with her other priorities. In the second instance, if the candidate aspires to a position in sales that does not require her to assert herself, you just might be barking up the wrong tree.

Another answer that ought to raise a red flag is if the candidate tells you that he hates when people say *no* to him. His ability to handle the rejection that is inevitable in any sales environment is a hugely important component of the job. The best way to eliminate the preponderance of *nos* in a sales environment is to simply stop asking for the sale. You won't get many *yeses* with that strategy, but you will eliminate the *nos*.

In the wonderful business parable *Animals Inc.*, Kenneth Tucker and Vandana Allman write of Lily the sheep:

"The problem was that Lily was too sheepish, which is the primary occupational hazard faced by most sheep. If she had started the job with any confidence it quickly would have disappeared. But since she had absolutely no confidence in her ability to sell she had none to lose. As the days passed it became increasingly difficult for her to pick up the phone to face more rejection. 'I can't make calls today,' she would tell Princess. 'I slipped and broke my voice last night.' Or, 'I can't dial any calls today, I cracked a hoof.' Or, 'I can't come to work today, I'm having a bad hair day over my entire body.'"

As extreme as that may seem, I challenge you to look at your own poor to mid-level sales performers and see how infrequently they specifically ask for the sale. What many of them do is to clerk the sale and, as a consequence of being present during business hours and catering to incoming customers as necessary, they invariably get some sales. It is the difference between "clerking" and "selling" and, if they are anything like Lily the sheep, they may have just a few too many "bad hair days" for the health of your business.

If the candidate answers the question by saying that she worries about not knowing enough about the product, not having a client book, not having any sales experience, etc., this presents a great opportunity for you to explain why you advertised for candidates without sales experience and what your company will do to help get her up to speed in those areas. Again, do you want to hire a squirrel or train a horse?

We should embrace and welcome concerns that have to do with things that can be taught, learned and experienced. We should not dismiss or take lightly those issues that relate to wiring and/or the willingness to embrace the retail culture (hours, etc.).

What do you think the primary role of a salesperson is?

In its most pared down manner, this is the central question that needs to be answered. Understanding that the role of a salesperson is "to sell" is about as important as anything else that we might hear from a candidate.

If the answer to this question turns out to be some variation of "providing great service" or "having great product knowledge" or "being nice to people," etc., then your work is far from done and you must continue to probe to see if she understands that in your world the salesperson's job is to sell *and* to provide all of the aforementioned necessities of service, product knowledge, etc. All of the great attributes are of little consequence if the salesperson doesn't understand that their primary role is to drive business.

The very notion that salespeople are expected to *sell stuff*, not just *clerk stuff*, is a foreign concept to the majority of people who are actually employed in sales today.

One of the things that I did in a previous position in the jewelry business was to undertake what I will loosely term as retailer interventions. The visits to the retail stores could last anywhere from a few hours to a couple of days. They were generally undertaken when an account was either struggling with the brand I was then working with, or if we believed that by spending some quality time in the store there was a strong opportunity to take our business together to a whole new level.

While the *intervention* focused on a myriad of disciplines to include marketing, the retail environment, compensation, product, etc., the single most telling aspect of the visits for me was the one-on-one conversations with the individual salespeople. It never ceased to amaze me how open and honest salespeople could be with a virtual stranger and I usually got a goldmine of information from these meetings with just a few prepared questions coupled with the willingness to listen to the salespeople.

On one such visit, I brought an account manager from our company to witness his first such *intervention*. Over the course of a few hours in the retail store, I interviewed all seven of the salespeople to better understand how the team was shaped and to figure out what we might do to positively impact the business.

At one stage in the interview process we met with two people back to back who represented, in a microcosm, the best and worst of, not just hiring practices, but also the insane way we sometimes view employee performance and potential. The first of the two employees was a very attractive, mid-twenties, young woman who was, according to the owner of the business, "as sweet as pie" and "very socially connected." Not surprisingly, she was very nicely dressed, very articulate and, on first blush, about the perfect employee. The employee that followed was probably twenty years older. She was not dressed nearly as stylishly as her younger colleague and she didn't come across as terribly articulate, nor did anyone suggest to me in advance that she was sweet as pie or particularly well connected.

The manner in which the two employees answered my questions revealed a depth of understanding that had nothing to do with experience and everything to do with inherent wiring (or lack thereof) for sales. The one question that really underscored the divide was when I asked each to describe, *in the fewest number of words*, the primary role of a salesperson.

I like to ask that question because it reveals so much about the salesperson's wiring. Because the question is so direct, it generally forces a response that is closer to the core of who the person is than if I were to ask it in a more general manner. The second very important reason for asking the question is that it can be quite telling in letting me know whether the person is a good listener or not—an absolutely essential characteristic in great sales performers. In particular, I place an emphasis on "in the fewest number of words..." for good reason. I am looking for a short, concise indication of what that person's natural wiring is.

When I asked the question of the young woman, who had been an employee of that store for about three years, she spoke at great length about giving the customer a great experience, treating them right, not pressuring them to buy, etc., etc. I deliberately let her expound to her heart's content in answering the question and the more she spoke the more I understood that she was simply not a natural salesperson.

The same question posed to her colleague elicited the most concise and direct answer I have ever gotten when asking that question. She said, quite simply, "to sell, profitably." I was completely won over by her answer and by her energy and level of engagement in the process. My instinct about the two ladies was later proven to be correct when I learned that the young woman sold $300k per year and her "less connected" colleague sold $1.1 million.

I am sure that there was a salary discrepancy between the two ladies but I doubt that it reflected the chasm in productivity. My own experience in situations like this often shows that there might be salary differences of $15k–$20k and that the owner of the store engages in a strange, if subconscious, rationalization that the younger woman "just doesn't cost that much," so it's okay if she doesn't produce as much as her colleague. Plus, of course, there's the sweet and connected factor to be considered!

Rather than accept the cost of one employee versus the other as "only" $15k or $20k, let's look at the numbers a little differently. Both women work in the same store, they have, ostensibly, the same opportunity to succeed, they work with the same brands, the same general compensation system, and they work for the same owner. In a perfect world, they would both be very productive salespeople. The reality, however, is that one employee produces $1.1 million in annual sales while the second employee produces $300k in sales. That's a whopping $800k difference per year, not the $15k or $20k salary difference that appears to be, on the surface, not that bad a deal.

The reason for the $800k difference is that one lady is a professional salesperson and the other is not. The sales wiring versus the non-sales wiring results in the more productive employee closing a much higher percentage of sales, at a higher average ticket per transaction, with better up-sell and cross-sell successes and a far more developed and successful client book.

If you were to carry those difference across a two-year period (a period of time that many non-producers manage to hang around), that difference in performance between the two ladies becomes $1.6m. Furthermore, if you had two of those unproductive employees who both stuck around for two years, the difference between a top producer and two non-producers over that period of time would be $3.2 million. That is pure lost business as a result of putting less-than-stellar salespeople in front of your customers and prospects day in and day out and losing the opportunities one customer at a time.

Reasonable people can debate what the situation might be if the above scenario was to have three great producers instead of one great salesperson and two poor salespeople. Perhaps you wouldn't have a $1.1 million x 3, as there can be a variety of others factors that come into play (length of tenure, such that one person's customer base is bigger than another's, market size, inventory levels, capital to buy the necessary goods, etc.) but where there can be no disagreement is that the return for the store would be infinitely more robust if poor salespeople were replaced by productive salespeople.

A number of years ago I taught a class at an industry trade conference entitled *The Lost Business Model*. To a large extent, it was an expanded version of the above scenario and it challenged retailers to think about the costs of poor producers in terms of lost business, instead of the much smaller issue of salary discrepancy. I argued that for all the money spent on product, facilities, marketing, training, etc., in the final analysis, it all has to pass through a very telling filter called salespeople. If you get the personnel side of things right, you can look like a genius in the myriad other disciplines. If, on the other hand, you get that wrong, you will find yourself chasing shadows as you try to find the next great product innovation, the next great marketing plan, a great trainer or motivator, a new compensation system, etc. Do you ever notice how really smart coaches become dumb when they lose their best players or how smart previously dumb coaches become when they have great players?

In thinking about the scenario with the two salespeople, I am reminded of an old colleague of mine, John Mc Barron, who once said that there is no such thing as bad taste. "One either has taste, or one does not," John would often extol. To a large extent, he could have used the same principle and said that there is no such thing as a bad salesperson, one either is or one is not. It may not suit us to think that one either is, or is not, a salesperson (what about all those motivational speakers, trainers and gurus, who would have us believe that the right course, tape or seminar will serve as the light bulb moment for our dormant people?) but there is a powerful truth in that.

At a conference in 2011, the company I was working with decided to put a real push on getting salespeople to sign up to be what we called "Champions." What that meant was that salespeople were committing to selling a certain amount of our branded products over the ensuing year and, in doing so, qualifying for Champion status. This Champion status was aspired to by many salespeople across numerous countries, but it was actually achieved by very few.

The drive to sign people up for Champion status at this particular conference was very successful, to the point that more than 400 people pledged to do whatever was necessary to become a Champion. Eleven weeks after the signups, and right in the midst of the Christmas season, when sales were at their zenith for the year, more than 100 of those people had not sold a single piece of our brand's product, not one. To put that into perspective, these "aspiring Champions" should have sold about 35–40 pieces of jewelry by that time in the season to have been tracking Champion status and yet they had sold nothing, not a piece.

In contemplating the disconnect, rather than question the motivation for those 100 to sign up for something that they were clearly not capable of accomplishing, I was reminded that if the sales wiring is not there, it just wasn't going to happen. The degree to which those salespeople had failed (not a single piece sold) points out the chasm between what one may believe oneself capable of and what one truly is capable of. The horses lined up to climb the trees but when the dust settled, the trees contained nothing but squirrels.

How would you go about building a client book?

It may strike you as unfair, perhaps even unrealistic, to ask someone without any sales experience to tell you how they would go about building a client book. And, to a certain degree, you would be correct. So why ask the question? Why broach the subject at all if you know that the candidate could not possibly have any knowledge of what is entailed in building a client book?

We ask the question because we want to see how the candidate thinks on his feet when the question is asked. Does the idea of being responsible for building a client book strike him as a foreign concept? Is he put off by that idea? Does that responsibility jive with his understanding of what being a salesperson is all about? Is he intuitive enough to guess at some of the things that he might be able to do to build a book?

We also ask the question to underscore the idea that building a client book is a central principle of becoming a sales professional in your company. It is communicated as one of the central tenets of sales professionalism and, while there is no expectation that a person coming into the company would have a book, you want them to know that they will be expected to begin working on it immediately. In asking this question, you might also be surprised to learn that the candidate has a rather extensive stable of friends and acquaintances from his own network, a consequence of being an active connector that could provide a good head start.

When I reference a "client book" it does not necessarily have to be an actual book. It could be, if that is your preferred option, but it might just as easily be anything from a CRM program to a well-organized box of index cards. Your company may already have a preferred method (and if you do not, it's time change that)—which is what your employees should use but, no matter what the system, having a client book for a salesperson should be as routine as getting dressed in the morning.

A candidate without sales experience should at least be able to ask questions about the process of building a book. He should, at the very least, express some interest and curiosity about what it means to build a book, how long it could take, and what tools might be available to help him get there. Asking this question should invoke a rich vein of conversation on a client development initiative that is absolutely essential in sales.

If you sense a little reluctance on the part of the candidate to embrace the idea of developing a client book, you should probe a little deeper. This is not a topic that you want to be ambiguous about.

What does active listening mean to you?

Without question, empathy, the ability and willingness and desire to listen to the customer, to hear what he or she is saying, to understand what he or she may want to communicate to you but may not be able to (because they don't know how to say it... ...because you haven't earned their trust yet!), to be able to read between the lines, to be able to understand on some basic level the fundamentals of body language, is one of the major requirements if one is to become a great sales professional.

Listening is simply not a skill that can be taught. If the candidate is a good listener, you will have uncovered one of the three major pillars of a great salesperson (along with Drive and Resilience). If the candidate is not a good listener he or she will never become great at sales. They might be the most silver-tongued, the most assertive, the most confident, and the most persuasive candidate you have ever encountered, but they will never become great at sales if they are not a good listener and, I make no apology for repeating myself on this point, you cannot teach someone to be a good listener. If they do not have empathy, it is not a learned skill or behavior. Ernest Hemmingway was quoted as saying, "I like to listen. I have learned a great deal from listening carefully. Most people never listen."

Ask the candidate to speak to you on the importance of listening. Determine whether there is sincerity and a passion in their response on the topic and ask yourself if it jives with your experience throughout the interview. Does this seem like a candidate who is really listening? Does she interrupt often? Does she actively listen? Do you find yourself having to repeat or rephrase questions?

If your salesperson is the hammer-wielding, nail seeking type, you will have found someone who might possess strong Drive and Resilience but who lacks Empathy. They are not that interested in hearing what the customer has to say. They are not really listening when the customer is communicating, verbally and nonverbally. They are oftentimes so wrapped up in their own story and in what they are going to say next, that they couldn't begin to pick up the important cues being communicated by the customer. They are too busy hammering nails to detect the nuances and they miss the many clues that the customer provides, because they are just too busy being "great salespeople" to listen.

I have seen many salespeople throughout my career who believe that they are the hammer to the customer's nail. They can appear to be successful, to the extent that they can be very good transactional salespeople. What they do not do is win the customer's confidence or loyalty and they tend not to be very good relationship builders. They often drive away solid prospects who otherwise would have happily engaged with someone who would have really listened to them.

It doesn't matter what the candidate's background is, professionally and/or academically when it comes to listening. If they have empathy and the capacity to be great listeners, they possess one of the most important tools in any great salesperson's arsenal.

Great listeners ask great questions. They ask great questions because they want to learn more about you, about the topic, about how they can help you. They tend to ask good open-ended questions: "Tell me about...would you describe...help me understand..." etc.

If it is true that one cannot become a great salesperson without the fundamental drive to get there, it is equally true that any real success in sales performance absolutely demands that the salesperson has good empathy—the willingness and the capacity to hear the customer.

The American philosopher, Mortimer Adler said, "Is anyone anywhere taught how to listen? How utterly amazing is the general assumption that the ability to listen well is a natural gift for which no training is required. How extraordinary is the fact that no effort is made anywhere in the whole educational process to help individuals learn how to listen well."

Adler's observation on the low priority placed on listening in academia or elsewhere is absolutely bang on. And, while I absolutely agree on the importance that he places on listening, where I would differ from Mr. Adler is in his inference that we can actually teach people to listen or to have empathy. I don't believe that we can teach empathy, but we can place an appropriate level of emphasis on it when hiring salespeople. As stated, it is one of the three pillars of sales wiring, alongside drive and resilience.

I believe I have a sufficient supply of empathy, and my *Caliper* test supports that contention, but there are still occasions, professionally and personally, when I am reminded of its importance and of my own shortcomings in that area.

On a trip to England a while back I had an experience in a taxi that stayed with me for all the wrong reasons. I was leaving my London hotel and I had decided that the best way to get to the airport was to take a taxi to Paddington Station and from there, take the Heathrow Express train to the airport. This, I reasoned, would save a good deal of money, as the taxi ride in from the airport was very expensive and it would also eliminate the likelihood of me hitting unexpected heavy traffic en route to the airport.

When I jumped in the taxi at the hotel and told the driver that I wanted to go Paddington Station, about a ten-minute drive, he became noticeably agitated. He started shaking his head and audibly lamented his lousy luck in getting me as a passenger. He had, apparently, been sitting in the taxi line at the hotel for an hour and a half in anticipation of a more lucrative airport ride.

As you might imagine, I was none too pleased at his unprofessionalism and his discourteous lament and I promptly responded to his mild tirade by assertively asking if he wanted me to get another taxi. He declined my offer and no more was said by either one of us for the duration of the tension-filled ride to the train station. My annoyance had abated by the time we arrived and, as a token of good will, I gave him a generous tip.

On the ensuing train ride to the airport, I began to think about the experience and I concluded that it was a classic case of two wrongs not making a right and, ultimately, a missed opportunity. With the benefit of hindsight, I still believed that the cabbie was out of order in showing his frustration over the shorter-than-hoped-for fare. I was a customer and, as such, I had no obligation to meet his agenda. It is not at all unusual to have hotel guests take trains to their respective destinations and he certainly violated the spirit of good will that I have very often found in taxi drivers in London.

On the other hand, I regretted that I had not been a little more understanding of his situation. It would have been a much better scenario for him if he had scored a fare to Heathrow or Gatwick airports and it was just the luck of the draw that he got me and my ten-minute journey to Paddington. Had I demonstrated a little more empathy, his experience and mine might have been greatly improved. Instead of a ride that was uncomfortable for both of us, we might have gotten to engage a little more and, quite frankly, it is even conceivable, had I enjoyed his company, that I might have suggested that he take me all the way to the airport.

We never had that opportunity because I didn't really listen to what he was saying, even if he was out of line in showing his agitation. My empathic meter was temporarily suspended and I never gave a moment's thought to the taxi driver's frustration. He had sat there for one and a half hours—and he would likely have to go back to the end of the line and start all over again with only a £7 fare to show for his investment of time.

A day or two earlier, on that very trip, I had been sharing a story with a colleague of mine about a taxi ride in London some years previous that was a great experience for me and, I suspect, for the driver. We were stuck in gridlock traffic, going nowhere fast, and the driver, who had been quite friendly to me up to that point, offered a challenge. He asked if I wanted to play a pop trivia game with him and, if I could answer three of five questions he would pose, he would comp the fare.

The long and short of it was that he and I had a great laugh, the traffic situation faded quickly from our minds and, in case you are wondering, I won the bet. As you might imagine, I insisted on paying him for the fare and I gave him a generous tip to boot. I had allowed him into my space; I had demonstrated good empathy. Instead of allowing myself to become frustrated by the traffic, I allowed the driver to engage with me and we were both better served for the interaction.

I thought about that previous taxi trip, in light of my recent exchange with the unhappy cab driver, and I wondered if we could have enjoyed a similar experience. If I had demonstrated a little more empathy and consideration for him—and I had been a little less aggrieved at his agitation—we might have found a way to connect and to have enjoyed a better experience. It didn't happen that day because his taxi meter and my empathy meter were both on short runs.

Rate Yourself on Optimism from 1–10...

In many respects this question serves a similar role as when we earlier asked the candidate to rate themselves on competitiveness scale. The act of giving oneself a grade, and then discussing why we elected that particular grade, can be very revealing. Does the candidate select a mid-level grade because she thinks that is a safe place to be? Does she rate herself a lower score and defend that by suggesting that she is a "realist" or a "pragmatist"? Does she score herself a 10 and proceed to tell us that everything will always come up roses if we only believe as much? Once again, there is no absolutely best answer to this question but it should make for a very interesting conversation.

Martin Seligman writes in *Learned Optimism*, "We all become momentarily helpless when we fail. The psychological wind is knocked out of us. We feel sad, the future looks dismal, and putting out any effort seems overwhelmingly difficult. Some people recover almost at once; all the symptoms of learned helplessness dissipate within hours. Others stay helpless for weeks or, if the failure is important enough, for months or longer." The preponderance of rejection in a sales environment does not fit well with a pessimistic demeanor. As we have discussed earlier, when a salesperson fears rejection, he is far less likely to ask for the sale. By doing so, he exposes himself to a kind of death by a thousand daggers. No one cut is fatal, but the sum total of repeated rejection compounds the stress and anxiety to the point where, as Seligman suggests, we are reluctant to put out much, if any effort at all.

Philip Delves Broughton writes in *The Art Of The Sale,* "By contrast, optimists succeed in sales, which leads to more optimism and more success. They feel the opposite of learned helplessness: learned optimism. Optimism and pessimism turn out to have a compounding effect on success in sales." When I think about the very best salespeople that I have worked with over the years, I would suggest that every single one of them can reasonably be described as an optimist. They have different styles, different personalities, different approaches to how they conducted themselves in sales, but every single one of them has an unfailing optimism that, despite the challenges and obstacles, they will be successful. When their level of performance does not meet their own high standards, they do not become consumed in the defeat. Rather, they remind themselves that they aren't going to make every sale or every goal and they proceed to tackle the next opportunity with great optimism.

Ask the candidate to support their self-grade with some stories and don't hesitate to respectfully challenge why a particular score was selected. For instance, if he gave himself a low score (towards pessimism), ask him why you should to hire him for sales without the optimism that is so essential to the sales psyche? If he scores himself a 10, ask him to speak to that grade so that you can determine if he really is a great optimist or whether he is telling you what he thinks you want to hear. As a reminder, no one question can appropriately determine whether a candidate will be right for sales or not but each question helps to build a picture. If there is a strong thread of consistency across the candidate's answers, your decision will be much easier to make. If you find that the candidate is erratic and inconsistent with his answers, you are probably best to move along and look at other options.

The 12 Questions for Sales Candidates Without Experience

- What Do You Think You Would Most Enjoy About Sales?
- Describe A Situation When An Idea Of Yours Was Rejected And Tell Me How You Felt About That...
- What Are Your Favorite Activities Outside Of Work?
- Why Do You Think I Should Hire Someone With No Sales Experience?
- Tell Me About A Failure Of Yours...
- When You Are Shopping, What Kind Of Salesperson Impresses You?
- On A Scale Of 1-10, How Competitive Are You?
- What Aspects Of Sales Do You Think Would Be Most Challenging For You?
- What Do You Think The Primary Role Of A Salesperson Is?
- How Would You Go About Building A Client Book?
- What Does Active Listening Mean To You?
- Rate Yourself On Optimism from 1-10...

The interview questions can serve multiple purposes. In the first instance, they enable you to peel back the layers of convention and conditioning associated with standard interviews, to the extent that you really begin to get at the inherent wiring of the candidate. Secondly, all of the questions can reasonably be asked and, more importantly, answered by someone who does not have sales experience. One might suggest that there is a third element to the questions, insofar as they serve as a primer to let the candidate know what your definition of a salesperson is. While there may be some merit to that school of thought, I am reluctant to embrace its value completely, believing that convincing someone that it takes a squirrel to climb a tree does not make them a squirrel.

I should take a minute to remind the reader that the questions are constructed to help uncover the inherent wiring of a candidate without sales experience. That said, some of the questions can serve equally well for candidates with experience. Remember, the questions should be accompanied by your prepared questions to review the job and/or academic history, as defined by the resume (is it real and is it relevant?) and also by your prepared questions, to determine whether the candidate is a good fit in your culture. If the candidate does well in potential sales wiring and in your resume discussion, but does not seem to fit your culture, that should be an important mitigating factor in the hiring decision.

The last point I want to make is that the effectiveness of the questions is tied directly into your willingness to state them clearly, reiterate them when necessary, and to really listen to the answers provided by the candidate. Refrain from interjecting or interrupting unless it is to refocus a candidate who is not answering the question you asked.

Select Questions for
"Experienced" Candidates

S o, you may ask, what questions should you ask of candidates who have previous sales experience? In short, what I am really saying about "experienced" sales candidates is to not infer any sales competence as a consequence of their having been employed in a sales role previously (whether that was one year or ten years) and to undertake the very same process of determining whether they have the appropriate wiring for sales as you would with an inexperienced candidate. Again, understand that the majority of people currently employed in sales should be doing some other kind of work. By all means interview experienced candidates; just don't give them credit, where none may be warranted, for having survived in sales for some number of years. Explore the resume to see if it is real and relevant and ask the questions you need to ask to determine whether there could be a good culture fit.

The following set of questions can be asked of "experienced" candidates. They include some of the very same questions we would ask of candidates without experience and, where appropriate, I have slightly altered some questions and added some others. For instance, *Tell Me How You Would Go About Building A Client Book* is changed to *Tell Me About Your Client Book*. In that example, the candidate should be able to speak to what they have done, or are currently doing, to drive customer development initiatives.

There should be a higher bar for a candidate with sales experience on this question as they have, supposedly, made a living in sales and they really should have figured this stuff out by now. Some of the questions are exactly the same as the previous list because they are every bit as relevant for candidates with experience. For instance, *What Are Your Favorite Activities Outside of Work?* and *Tell Me About A Failure of Yours* are important questions that are not impacted by someone's sales experience, or lack thereof. There are also some very specific questions included to really get at the specificity of the "experienced" candidate's wiring. Questions such as *Describe A recent Sale Where You Had a Significant Influence On the Customer's Decision to Buy* and *How Do You Typically Handle Price Resistance From A Customer?* are very specific and can clearly only be answered by someone with sales experience.

What do you most enjoy about sales?

This is another way of asking the candidate to define what selling really means to them. We are looking to hear about traits and characteristics and, where possible, examples of particular sales that were made by the candidate. What we do not want to hear in answer to this question is a lot of filler: "I love working with people...I love selling beautiful products, etc." If we do not hear sales-specific answers to this question then perhaps the candidate is not wired for sales.

When I ask great salespeople what they love about their jobs, I often hear them boast about how they love taking care of their customers, about how excited they are to be a part of their customers' lives, often attending important events in their customers' calendars such as weddings, christenings and other important occasions. Great salespeople find a way to make an emotional connection with their customers. They invest of themselves and they earn the right to establish a relationship that is infinitely more than simply "transactional" in nature.

A couple of years ago I was visiting a jewelry store in Dallas, Texas. The purpose of my visit was to attempt to understand why the brand

I was working with at that time was not enjoying better sell-through success. As I mentioned earlier in the book, an important part of these visits, or interventions, as I sometimes called them, was to meet with each member of the sales team to understand why they were, or were not, successful selling the brand.

As I proceeded through the various interviews, I encountered a particular salesperson. I will call her Sandra. I asked Sandra to share with me a story or two of successes she had selling the brand. Sandra, in a very nonchalant manner, shrugged her shoulders and told me that she really didn't sell the brand very much and she volunteered a litany of reasons as to why that was the case. After a couple of minutes of gentle prodding and cajoling, she finally remembered a particular sale that she agreed to share with me. As Sandra started to tell me the story, she broke down in tears.

After composing herself, Sandra proceeded to tell me the story of a young soldier named Emidio Zanetti. Emidio, it transpired, had shown up in her store some months previous from his Forth Worth home. She remembered that Emidio had been a little nervous, as he had little to no experience shopping in jewelry stores, and certainly no experience whatsoever buying an engagement ring, the reason for his visit that day. He told Sandra that he had done some research online and that he was quite certain that he wanted to buy this particular brand of diamond for his significant other.

At one point in their conversation, Sandra asked Emidio about the tattoos on his arm. Emidio told Sandra that he had served in the military and the names tattooed on his arm were those of his friends that he had lost during his tours of duty. He then directed Sandra's attention to one name in particular and he mentioned that this particular name was that of his best friend. Emidio told Sandra that when he returned from his tour of duty, he had made a point to visit with the young widow of his fallen friend and comrade and, over a period of time, they had fallen in love.

When Emidio decided that it was time for him to ask the young widow to marry him, he was determined to get his intended the very best engagement ring he could afford. Emidio, quite simply, was so in awe of what his future wife had already gone through in her young life that he wanted to do something quite magical for her.

Emidio's research led him to this particular diamond brand and, ultimately, into that store. He wanted his intended to have the very best that money could buy and he was determined to get it for her. Emidio paid over $16,000 to buy the engagement ring from a store that he had never previously set foot in, and from a salesperson he had never before met.

The young soldier had given two phenomenal gifts to Sandra that day and she had remembered them only after considerable prodding and encouragement from me. In the first instance, Emidio had given her a $16,000 sale, no small undertaking in that or any jewelry store. Perhaps even more importantly, he had given her the gift of a powerfully emotive story that should have opened her eyes beyond the narrow confines of her own inhibitions and biases.

Without ever intending to do so, Emidio had delivered the single best example of how we are all driven to do things that might, with the help of a little "cognitive reasoning" or a little "rationalization" seem very illogical. He had spent, what was for him, and for many people, an exorbitant sum of money to make the very best statement he could make for his bride-to-be.

On the surface, this young man was hardly the kind of customer that this particular jewelry store targeted. In fact, why would they? People like him surely did not earn enough money to buy at that store and, even if they did, they could certainly never spend the kind of money necessary to buy one of their diamond rings. Emidio's visit and purchase was unexpected and it did not conform to any of the stereotypes that we envision for who might and might not purchase in our fine stores.

Sandra had so quickly forgotten a story that should have been a life's lesson for her. She had been quick to dismiss the relevance of the brand to her store and, remarkably, she had forgotten what the experience had meant to the young soldier. She had been telling my colleague and I how the brand was just a little too expensive, and how most of her customers were "not likely to spend that kind money" to buy it. She was, in fact, committing two major sins: she was spending from her own pocket, something we see over and over again with weak salespeople, and she was forgetting that people are very often moved to act in seemingly illogical ways when they are emotionally invested.

When I met the management team of that business the following day, I started by asking them if they knew who Emidio Zanetti was. They made a couple of wise-cracks about racecar drivers and what not, but it was clear that this powerful story had not made their radar at all, let alone served to move them beyond their own narrow stereotypes of who their target customer was.

They should have used young Emidio as the best example of how not to pre-judge your customers, how not to profile them and about how their salespeople should always expect the best of every prospect who walks through their doors. They should have reached out to Emidio to find a way to pay tribute to him and to publicly thank him for his service and for his business. Instead, they revealed that they knew nothing at all of Emidio and the many valuable lessons from his visit were, sadly, lost.

Emidio's story could move Sandra to tears months after she had met him, but only with our coaxing and prodding. Otherwise, it took its place in the dark recesses of her mind, destined to live in obscurity with the rest of her transactions and interactions.

I wish that I could say that Sandra was an exception. I wish I could believe that the majority of salespeople would have understood the magnitude of that story and would have been moved by it. The reality, unfortunately, is that Sandra is not an exception. In fact, she might be better than most as she was, at least on a subconscious level, capable of being moved to tears in recalling and retelling the story. She was, however, also largely disconnected from the responsibilities and opportunities presented as a retail salesperson day in and day out. Sandra is one of the 60% or so of salespeople who somehow manage to eke out a living doing a job that they are completely unsuited to do.

Describe a situation when an idea of yours was rejected and tell me how you felt about that...

This is the same question that was posed to the candidate without experience. We are trying to understand if he or she can readily recall situations (storytelling) of relevance and whether she demonstrates sufficient resilience in overcoming the disappointment. I am always surprised at the level of detail that some folks will get into when talking about their lives and experiences with a complete stranger. If the candidate has the capacity—and the humility—to share an important experience when they were rejected, you can learn a great deal about his or her resilience. Listening carefully to how they responded to that rejection and by carefully observing the body language you can gauge whether the body language aligns with the candidate's narrative. While the candidate may tell you that he or she found the rejection to be a great learning experience, what the body language may tell you is that they hold a seething anger about the rejection. Of course, that presumes that the candidate is forthcoming enough to tap into a matter that evokes emotion. If they are unwilling or unable to do that, then you might have a different issue entirely—unless, of course, you believe that he or she is the one human being who has not faced some rejection in his or her life.

What we would like to hear is a real story about a matter that did, in fact, cause some consternation, but which ultimately served to show that the candidate has the capacity to suffer rejection without becoming paralyzed by it. In describing stocks traders, Paul Sullivan writes in Clutch, "Any trader who made a lot of money would whistle his way into the office the next day, but that did not make him a great trader. The best ones were the ones who could lose a lot of money and still be ready to trade when the markets opened again. Their common trait was that they didn't like to fail, which is different from disliking losing. All traders lose at some point, but it doesn't mean they failed. It means they lost on a particular day."

What are your favorite activities outside of work?

This question is as relevant to someone with sales experience as to someone without. We still need to understand what activities and interests she is drawn to when she has personal time and to understand whether those choices are consistent with a desire to be connected to people and action, or less connected to people and more sedentary in nature. As Kosslyn and Miller write in *Top Brain, Bottom Brain,*

"If your genes incline you toward a very active temperament, you will probably engage in sports and take trips that involve an element of adventure—perhaps going rock climbing on a very challenging mountain face or rafting down rapids. But if your genes incline you to have a more passive temperament, you will likely gravitate toward more laid-back pursuits—reading or gardening, for example."

Again, having an interest that is not overly social, which does not put the candidate around other people, is not in and of itself an issue. If, however, it represents a necessary and needed escape from a work situation that does not align with that person's wiring and comfort level, then it should be viewed with some degree of caution.

Describe a recent sale where you had a significant influence on the customer's decision to buy...

This ought to be a very easy question for a salesperson with experience to answer. Whether the story is on message and believable or not is another matter entirely. As with most of the questions, we are looking for specificity in the candidate's response. We want to know the circumstances surrounding the exchange with the customer. We want to hear what the challenges were and how those challenges were overcome by the salesperson. We want to know specifically how the salesperson influenced the outcome and convinced the customer to make a buying decision. The more detail they can provide the better.

What we are clearly not looking for is a transaction that seemed to happen without significant influence or persuasion on the part of the salesperson. The telling of specific transactions that seem to have been little influenced by actions by the salesperson have value only to the extent that they may reveal a lack of understanding of the sales process by the candidate. Sometimes this question elicits a story of a large sale in the belief that the scale itself is exciting, but absent specific influencers from the candidate.

Answers that offer specifics—what was said, what was done, challenges that were overcome, suggestions made by the salesperson that influenced the customer's buying decision—give a much greater insight into the fundamental awareness by the candidate of the actual sales process.

If you are interviewing an "experienced" candidate and he or she cannot readily recall specific examples of having influenced some sales, you are probably in the company of a clerk and you might be best served looking elsewhere.

Tell me about a failure of yours...

It is not possible to be great in sales unless you have the capacity to recover from failure. If you can look at your failures and see them as learning opportunities then you will have established a very important ingredient in the makeup of a great sales producer.

We also ask this question because we want to know how well the candidate connects storytelling (a hugely important element in sales) with her own personal disappointments. In listening to the candidate talking about her failure, we want to closely observe the body language to determine whether there is alignment or disconnect between what she is saying and what she is nonverbally communicating.

We would ideally like the candidate to tap into an important experience in her life or career and we want her to speak honestly to that failure in such a way as to convince you that she has the intellect to recognize and connect that experience with the question, and the emotional resolve to overcome it.

Tell me about the best salesperson you have ever worked with...

What we are looking for with this question is another version of the things that the candidate values when they think about the qualities of a salesperson. If the candidate begins to discuss strong service orientation, product knowledge and friendliness, instead of sales accomplishments, client-development initiatives or delivering great customer solutions, then we ought to pay attention and peel a few more layers from that particular onion.

Some years ago I was interviewing a candidate for a retail store operated by one of my clients. Victoria had asked me to help her with the interview process as, beyond the normally big stakes involved in any hire, she was considering relocating the candidate from Las Vegas to Tucson.

The candidate's credentials had been submitted by an industry recruiter and, as well as having a strong branded retail pedigree, the candidate was also bilingual—an important factor with her store located in Arizona. By any reasonable measure, the candidate appeared to be a great fit and there was a good deal of anticipation on Victoria's part that this might be the right hire for her store.

After the initial few minutes of small talk, we began the interview proper. Before long, it became apparent that not only had the candidate not given much thought to the potentially huge matter of relocation, but he also struggled to answer any specific questions that had to do with his wiring and performance as a salesperson. Try as we might, we simply could not get him to speak to any of the relevant traits or the wiring that might indicate that he possessed the requisite sales skills to support his resume and experience.

Almost as a last resort, and in an effort to understand why any recruiter would have submitted this candidate for consideration, I asked him to describe the best salesperson he had ever worked with. As he started to describe his former colleague, I became momentarily excited that we might finally have hit upon some relevant sales wiring.

He told us how this lady had always found a way to get herself involved in the community through local charitable events, etc. He then described how she was full of energy and how very personable she had been.

Against my better instincts, I found myself rooting hard for him to somehow bring his story back to the retail store. I wanted to hear how his former colleague's efforts to engage with the community had been responsible for her great relationship building and how those relationships, eventually, paid dividends for the business in real and sustainable sales.

Alas, we heard no such thing. He was unable to make the connection between the activities of his former colleague and her ability to tap into those contacts to benefit her store. He admired what she did without ever understanding why what she did mattered or connected to her job as a salesperson. I have no doubt that his colleague was able to connect her activities to her store's business, but I was equally certain that our interviewee didn't understand that.

When a candidate answers this question we want to hear from him that the person he is describing has the requisite qualities and the inherent wiring that we hope he himself has, even if he cannot articulate that when describing himself.

If he talks about a person's drive, or their ability to close sales, or their competitiveness, then it opens the door for the interviewer to discuss those important and very relevant attributes with the candidate. If, like our friend in Las Vegas, they fail to recognize how these great characteristics and activities ultimately pay off for the retail store, then what we really have is the illusion of competence and fit.

On A Scale of 1–10, How Competitive Are You?

Once again, asking this question of a candidate with sales experience is every bit as important as asking it of a candidate without sales experience. In the later scenario, we are trying, in the absence of a sales history, to deduce whether there is an inherent competitive drive. Asking this question of an experienced sales candidate enables you to cross-check his answer against tangible examples that speak to his stated competitive bent. Of course, if the candidate gives himself a low score on competitiveness, this conversation—and the interview itself—should be short.

It is not at all unusual for a sales candidate to submit a resume that speaks to everything a salesperson could do except selling. If you have such a resume—and you still committed to the interview—ask the candidate to reconcile his stated competitiveness against a resume that is short of tangible accomplishments.

We would like the candidate to give himself a high score and support that self-assessment with specific examples of accomplishments from his history.

What aspects of sales are most challenging for you?

The candidate can go any number of directions with this question but, no matter which way she takes it, we are looking for authenticity and relevance in her response. If we hear that she hates to come across to her prospects and customers as pushy, or that she doesn't like the pressure of sales goals, or that she suffers from anxiety every time she is asked to deliver sales goals, this is not a good sign. What she may really want is an environment where everyone gets along well and where no one has to concern themselves with meeting sales goals, up-selling or cross-selling, or any other type of sales initiative. She may really want a clerking position, absent the pressures and anxieties that come with a performance environment.

If, on the other hand, she stresses that there are just never enough hours in the day to get everything done, or that she wishes that the store foot traffic could be better spread across opening hours to allow her to take care of more customers, or that she sometimes becomes frustrated when she can't convince the customer to make a purchasing decision that day, then that is likely someone with strong sales wiring.

What we need to hear are frustrations that are tied into her aspiration to be a great sales professional, not anxieties about having to produce sales. As obvious as that statement is, we already know that there are as many as 60% of people employed in sales who are not cut out for selling. We also know, according to Gallup, that 70% of people in the United States are not engaged in their work. That means that a great many people who are currently employed in sales either do not have the essential wiring to perform that role at a high level, or if they do have the wiring, they lack the interest and commitment to be there. Rosabeth Moss Kanter writes in *Confidence*, "Psychologists use the term 'defensive pessimism' to describe the way some people set low expectations to cope with anxiety in risky situations. This set of people is not trying to make excuses or deny responsibility; they just prefer to expect failure, so as not to be totally debilitated by anxiety about whether they can meet a lofty goal."

In short, you want to hear the candidate share frustrations and challenges that are tied into her desire to be a better salesperson, not a candidate who shares frustrations and challenges about being a salesperson. There is nothing subtle about the difference between the two of those things and the costs of getting it wrong can be exorbitant.

What do you think the primary role of a salesperson is?

In an ideal world, this question would be answered the same way I described in this question under the inexperienced candidate questions: "To sell profitably." Accepting that such an answer might be a tad optimistic, we nonetheless would like to hear an answer that speaks to sales wiring and not a response that invokes all the standard rhetoric: having great product knowledge, providing great customer service, knowing the store's procedures, etc. We need to hear language that speaks to actual selling, meeting goals, driving business and relationship building. If the candidate tells you that she thinks her role is to not be too pushy, then you should *"call Houston,"* because you just might have a problem.

Tell me about your client book...

Stephanie, a retailer friend of mine, was once lamenting the challenges of finding great salespeople. Her search for great sales talent all too often came up empty, and she found herself in an endless and frustrating cycle of interviewing/hiring/training/firing.

She conceded that she was not a good interviewer and she confessed that she could not determine during the interview whether the candidate was just a good interviewer, looking and sounding the part and saying and doing all the right things, only to find out, after it was too late, that the interview itself was the candidate's best work. "How do I know whether that person will be good or not?" she asked.

As I have discussed throughout the course of this book, there are ways to significantly increase the odds of making the right hire and employing real difference-makers. The hiring process is not, and never will be an exact science; we are going to make mistakes, we are going to engage in wishful thinking with some of our hires, and we will miss potentially great people because of our own style of interviewing and because of the inherent biases that we bring into the process.

My advice to Stephanie, after a brief admonition on why her entire hiring process ought to be reviewed (the proof was very much in that pudding!) was that if she was interviewing an experienced salesperson—and that was exactly what she had been doing—that the single most important question to ask that candidate is *Tell me about your client book!*

Whether the candidate has one year's experience or ten years worth of experience, they should absolutely have a client book and they should be able to talk about it. This question is, for me, the single most important question that we can ask of an experienced sales candidate to determine whether they are the real deal or not. If the candidate does not have a client book—if they haven't figured that out in one or in ten years—then I am convinced that you are, in all likelihood, not looking at a person with the essential wiring to be a sales driver. Salespeople who have the necessary wiring will intuitively engage in actions and activities towards relation building and client development.

Consistent with their own often-held belief that they are really independent operators working in your business (not all bad), great salespeople invest time and energy building their client book to drive business. Difference-makers do not sit around during quiet times wondering how they are going to make a living; they proactively reach out to their client base and they make things happen.

In 1986, I started working for Tiffany's in Chicago as a salesperson and I thought I had died and gone to Heaven. I was living in one of the greatest cities in the world; I was working for an icon company in the industry and I was surrounded by great products and an endless stream of willing buyers. It was a great situation for me and I loved every minute of that experience, hustling from customer to customer, engaging, laughing, listening and selling. We were so inundated with Japanese customers at that time that I even took *Berlitz* classes to learn some basic Japanese to help me to sell more.

In many respects, I felt like I couldn't miss; things had never been so much fun for me in retail. I felt certain that I was working as hard as anyone on the sales staff and I was destined to be the most successful salesperson on the team. I was wrong.

While I was working really hard, a number of my colleagues were working really smart. Those were, of course, the days before the internet, before emails, tweets, *Facebook*, and even before cell phones. While it was a very different time, there was a fundamental discipline then that is no different today and that is, of course, the need to effectively clientele.

Our store was located on Michigan Ave., in Chicago, and there were days in winter that were so bitterly cold, or snowy, that the weather would render the streets as close to a ghost town as a big city could possibly get. On those days, while some salespeople stood around discussing the previous evening's television shows, or waxed poetic about that year's hopes for the Cubs (still waxing as I write this) the two or three best salespeople were working their client books and generating business. They were writing notes, making phone calls and, ultimately, making sales, while others lamented their misfortune due to the lousy weather and the lack of customers coming through the door.

The realization that I could generate my own business through client development was one of my great light bulb moments. I saw an opportunity to control my own destiny and my obsession, from that moment on, was to build my own client book.

Once the light bulb illuminated in my head, I took every opportunity to make a note on my copy of the sales receipt, or the waybill, as we called it then, of anything and everything I had learned about that customer and/or his or her significant other in the course of our conversation. My quick notes would then be transferred into my client book over the weekend and a quick hand-written thank you note would be sent.

As the owner of rather deplorable handwriting, I cringe at the thought of how anyone ever read my notes, but there can be no doubt that the practice was a big factor in helping to wrestle control of my own sales destiny and it continues to be every bit as important today as it was then.

While the number of vehicles with which to communicate with our clients has greatly expanded, with social media, texts, etc., the premise, and perhaps even the power of a hand-written note, is still as important today as it was then, perhaps more so.

As a point of clarification, when I talk about client books, I am not saying that it has to be an actual book. It could be a book, a CRM, a box of index cards...same principle. That it is done is more important than what vehicle one uses to communicate with your customers. As I think about the very best salespeople that I have worked with, I can say that 100% of them had client books that were as important to them as any other tool in their professional lives.

What you are really asking the candidate to talk about is the very idea of client development and what role, if any, it plays in their professional life. This open-ended question should be a great topic of conversation if you have happened upon a great sales candidate. If it is not, then you are not talking to a real sales driver.

I once asked Teri Ramirez what percentage of her business came from repeat clients as a result of her clientelling efforts. Teri was the single best seller of *Hearts On Fire* diamonds in the world. She told me that 75% of all of her sales (I would guess she was selling $3m–$4m a year) were a result of her client-development efforts.

I believe in this question so strongly that I would make a "no" decision based on the candidate's response. If you are dealing with someone who has been in sales long enough to have figured this out, and they have not done so, I would not make that hire.

What does active listening mean to you?

Randy Larsen and David Buss write in Personality Psychology, Domains of Knowledge About Human Nature, "There's the legend of the three blind men who were presented with an elephant. They tried to figure out what the whole elephant was like. The first blind man approached cautiously; walking up to the elephant and putting his hands and then arms around the animal's leg, he proclaimed, 'Why, the whole elephant is much like a tree, slender and tall.' The second man grasped the trunk of the elephant and exclaimed, 'No, the whole elephant is more like a large snake.' The third blind man grasped the ear of the elephant and stated, 'You are both wrong; the whole elephant more closely resembles a fan.' The three blind men continued to argue with each other, insisting that his opinion of the whole elephant was the correct one. In a sense, each blind man had a piece of the truth, yet each failed to recognize that his perceptions of the elephant captured only a narrow part of the truth. Each failed to grasp the whole truth. Working together, however, the blind men could have assembled a reasonable understanding of the whole elephant."

I've long enjoyed that story as I believe it is an interesting parable in highlighting why salespeople must listen better, do a better job reading the customer's body language, and elicit better feedback from their customers so that they might better gauge what the whole elephant is really like.

Greenberg, Sweeney and Weinstein write in How To Hire And Develop Your Next Top Performer, "We define empathy as the ability to sense the reactions of other people. It is the ability to pick up the subtle clues and cues provided by others in order to accurately assess what they are thinking and feeling."

Get the candidate talking about the power of listening and gauge whether his story is consistent with what you have experienced throughout the interview. Has he demonstrated great listening skills? Was he able to pick up on your subtle clues and inferences? Did he understand your questions the first go around or did you have to restate questions over and again? You cannot teach someone to listen well and, as I have said over and again, you cannot become a great salesperson without empathy. This question is very important and you should never underestimate its relevance in your decision-making process.

Rate Yourself on Optimism from 1–10...

This question is every bit as relevant for a candidate with experience as it is for an inexperienced candidate. We need to fundamentally understand how he or she views the world and his or her role in it. If the candidate communicates an upbeat and optimistic view of her opportunities and experiences, she will likely adopt that same demeanor on the sales floor.

One of the challenges in listening to the candidate's response is to discern whether the optimism you are witnessing is a function of an interviewing tactic or if it does, in fact, reflect a broader attitude that might likely carry over into the workplace. A great way to understand that, like most of the questions, is to listen very closely to the stories that are being told throughout the course of the interview and decide whether they are consistent. For instance, if she rates herself a ten on the optimist scale, but you find that score to be at odds with the stories you have been hearing, believe the body of evidence, not the self-score.

While I am not married to the idea that the interview questions need to be asked in a particular order, I would suggest that it would be best to ask this question later in the interview. To ask it earlier, may actually prime the interviewee and it could materially influence his or her behavior throughout the interview. It wouldn't take a great deal of intuition to deduce that if I am being asked to rate myself as an optimist then it must be important to the interviewer. Thereafter, it wouldn't be difficult to have the candidate inject a little theater into the conversation by spinning as much of his or her storytelling in an optimistic manner.

Don't be misled into believing that optimists necessarily need to be shouting positive affirmations from atop the mountain. Many great salespeople have a quiet and steely optimism that enables them to navigate through their chosen profession and, in particular, recover quickly from the inevitable setbacks that retail throws at them every day. Daniel Goleman writes in *Emotional Intelligence*,

"Just why optimism makes such a difference in sales success speaks to the sense in which it is an emotionally intelligent attitude. Each no a salesperson gets is a small defeat. The emotional reaction to the defeat is crucial to the ability to marshal enough motivation to continue. As the no's mount up, morale can deteriorate, making it harder and harder to pick up the phone for the next call. Such rejection is especially hard to take for a pessimist who interprets it as meaning, 'I'm a failure at this; I'll never make a sale.'—an interpretation that is sure to trigger apathy and defeatism, if not depression. Optimists, on the other hand, tell themselves, 'I'm using the wrong approach,' or 'That last person was in a bad mood.' By seeing not themselves but something in the situation as the reason for their failure, they can change their approach in the next call. While the pessimist's mental set leads to despair, the optimist's spawns hope."

While a self-score from a candidate on the extremes, a one or two on the low end, or a nine or ten on the high end, makes for an obvious follow up question ("Tell me why..."), don't underestimate the value of a mid-score, such as five or six, as a catalyst for a great follow up conversation. You may find that the candidate sees himself as a pragmatist or a realist and, while he doesn't give himself a high score, he may have more of an optimist's wiring than he lets on. Or, for that matter, you may find that he sees himself as a mediocre performer, not deserving of a very low or a very high score.

To state the obvious, if the candidate scores himself as a one or two and that low score jives with what you have been gleaning throughout the interview, you should pat yourself on the head for having conducted a successful interview and wish the candidate well—someplace else!

How do you typically handle price resistance from a customer?

There are not that many retail businesses that offer a negotiable price but one such model, in reality if less so in principle, is the retail jewelry business and, more specifically, the selling of diamonds. Unless you are Tiffany or Cartier, a disproportionate number of independent retail jewelry stores still have a "make-me-an-offer" mindset when it comes to selling their wares. Any salesperson that has come out of that environment has, by definition, had many experiences dealing with customers looking for a discount.

There are many "great salespeople" who are just killing the business by practically giving the product away. They drive business by making sales, but at great cost to the store in margins and profitability. You are not a great salesperson if you have to discount a product to make a sale. Too many so-called sales stars believe that they have to give something to the customer and what they are really doing is hurting their own company, enabling the worst habits of their customers, and underscoring the skepticism that customers and prospects might have about the legitimacy of the store's pricing.

According to a Gallup study, engaged customers deliver a 23% premium over average customers, while customers who are not engaged deliver a 13% discount to average customers. To that end, it is imperative that your salespeople have the talent to emotionally engage with your customers and deliver value, not the lowest price. The sage of Omaha, Warren Buffet, said that "Price is what you pay, value is what you get." The best salespeople are adept at overcoming price resistance and delivering value to their customers.

Describe a recent situation when you did not make a sale that you expected to make and tell me what you might have done differently...

This question is related to the earlier question when we asked the candidate to describe a sale that she had positively influenced. It is another way of asking her to break down the sales process and to help reveal whether she has enough humility to know that she can learn as much from her failures as from her successes and the resilience to deal with the setback.

When I asked Jennifer Carusone about her sales frustrations, she told me that understanding why the customer said *no* was very important to her. She said that she needed to dissect the rejection and build upon it as a learning experience. Kanter writes in *Confidence*, "Everything can look like a failure in the middle. Winners redefine setbacks as detours en route to success, and they redouble their efforts to find a way around obstacles." Dave Padgett told me that he often has to mentally review the selling process in his head to make sure that he has executed all the basics. He is always learning, always improving.

If you ask a good salesperson to tell you about a lost sale, and what they might have done differently to have influenced a better outcome, they will readily draw from an array of interactions because they are always thinking about the sales process. They continually break the sales interaction down and seek to learn from their shortcomings. They also have math on their side, given that the very best of them have more customers walk out of the store empty-handed than they do having made a purchase. That is a given in the vast majority of retail environments, where even the top salespeople might be closing no more than 30% of their prospects.

Select Questions for "Experienced" Candidates

- **What Do You Most Enjoy About Sales?**
- **Describe A Situation When An Idea Of Yours Was Rejected And Tell Me How You Felt About That...**
- **What Are Your Favorite Activities Outside Of Work?**
- **Describe A Recent Sale Where You Had A Significant Influence On The Customer's Decision To Buy...**
- **Tell Me About A Failure Of Yours...**
- **Tell Me About The Best Salesperson You Have Every Worked With...**
- **On A Scale Of 1–10, How Competitive Are You?**
- **What Aspects Of Sales Are Most Challenging For You?**
- **What Do You Think The Primary Role Of A Salesperson Is?**
- **Tell Me About Your Client Book...**
- **What Does Active Listening Mean To You?**
- **Rate Yourself On Optimism From 1–10...**
- **How Do You Typically Handle Price Resistance From A Customer?**
- **Describe A Recent Situation When You Did Not Make A Sale That... You Expected To Make And Tell Me What You Might Have Done Differently...**

Constantly Look for Talent

"I look to the future because that's where I'm going to spend the rest of my life." George Burns

The best run businesses are always on the lookout for great talent. They do not wait until they have an opening before beginning the search. If the biggest issue a company has is an overabundance of great talent, then that business is probably a top-performing company. Overloading with great talent, however, is much easier said than done. In fact, in thirty years of business, I have never once encountered a company that was so overly laden with great talent that it couldn't accommodate a superstar. However, if proactive talent activities are successfully implemented, they create the kind of dilemma that most business owners would love to have.

In a sales environment, where productivity is the lifeblood of the company, it has to be a survival of the fittest. There are going to be occasions when some good people are going to have to be moved on and that is never an easy thing to do. Those people are often loyal, long-term colleagues and friends. They may have been with you through thick and thin and you may have come to view them as a part of your family. That said, if you want to prioritize the health of the business and your obligation to your entire team, then turnover of poor-performing salespeople is a necessary evil.

In the end, people who are not wired for sales often find themselves a job that is a much better fit outside of sales. After years of poor performance, and sometimes traumatic separations, from long-term places of employment, they ultimately realize that they are more suited to other types of work. It could even be in retail stores, but just not selling. They are usually the last to see how ill-fitting a sales job is for their makeup and personality and that moment of clarity generally doesn't come until after they are removed from the environment.

As Levin and Rosse write in *Talent Flow*, "Simply minimizing turnover among employees is as poor a way to create a high-performing organization as striving to keep every person you know as a lifelong friend would be to create an enjoyable set of friendships. You don't have a goal of making everyone you meet a lifelong friend. It makes no sense to try to retain every employee you ever hired. Instead, you need an approach to retention that will create sustained talent flow." Do not wait until you have an opening to start looking for talented salespeople. It is a recipe for mediocrity in your team and in your business.

Assessment Companies

It is my sincere hope that this book will help you to become much better with your talent management but, no matter how skilled you become in this process, I cannot stress strongly enough that you should align yourself with an assessment company to help identify the appropriate traits and characteristics for your intended hires.

Herrenkohl writes in *How To Hire A-Players*, "Assessment tools provide an additional benefit. They temper your natural tendency to be charmed by certain candidates and pursue them despite their weaknesses. I know seasoned sales executives who refuse to interview any salespeople until they have completed an online sales assessment. These executives have made too many hiring mistakes based solely on initial impressions and 'gut instincts.' They like the fact that assessment tools inject objectivity about candidates into the interview process."

If you are not already using such a company, I have listed the contact information for a select few here. Do a little homework and interview some of these companies to see who might be the best fit for your business. Having selected a company, one of the first things you should do is to have your best people profiled. That will enable the assessment company to build a profile for your ideal candidates ongoing. If you do not have a superstar on your team currently, most assessment companies should still be able to interview you to determine what the essential qualities are in a salesperson for your store and to create a profile accordingly.

A last word on assessment companies before I move on: do not select one because it is the cheapest. No matter how expensive a given company seems to be, it pales in comparison to the cost of making a wrong hire.

- **Hogan**:   hoganassessments.com
- **PDI Ninth House:**   pdinh.com
- **PDP:**   pdpnet.com
- **Caliper:**   calipercorp.com
- **SHL:**   shl.com
- **Disc:**   discpersonalitytesting.com

Summary

"If you don't know where you are going any road will get you there."
Anonymous

If you want better results from your hiring practices you need to adopt a different approach to your talent management. This starts with an acceptance that not everyone can sell and that you cannot train the essential wiring to do so into someone who does not have the inherent drive to sell.

You should also know that experience is not only overrated but may, in fact, be a smokescreen that creates the illusion of sales competence where little to none exists. The opposite side of that coin, of course, is that there are people in all walks of life—many of them far removed from sales—who do have the wiring to be successful in sales, if we are willing to open our eyes and look at candidates from other professions. I know of really great salespeople who were previously employed as bartenders, schoolteachers, DJs, even a ballet dancer.

What is absolutely essential is that whomever you do decide to hire must have the essential wiring that includes *Drive, Empathy* and *Resilience.* Those traits alone do not ensure a successful hire, as the new hire must be right for your culture and he or she must have the necessary work ethic and character to meet your standards, but those attributes, absent *Drive, Empathy* and *Resilience* are simply not enough to make a great salesperson, or even a good salesperson.

Once you have expanded your options to include candidates without sales experience, it is important to change the way you interview. Having a structured process is essential to understand whether the wiring is present. By asking the 12 questions designed to uncover the candidates' traits (or the questions designed for candidates with sales experience), and by seeking to understand whether the candidate is right for your culture and whether he or she has a personal ethic and character that fits your needs will greatly improve your hiring proficiency.

As you interview candidates, remind yourself that people with great sales wiring (experienced or inexperienced) can be difficult to manage. The traits that make them successful drivers can be slightly off-putting to an interviewer, who might be more comfortable hiring people that he feels "great chemistry" with. The advertising icon, David Ogilvy wrote in *Confessions of an Advertising Man*, "Our business needs massive transfusions of talent...and talent, I believe, is most likely to be found among nonconformists, dissenters, and rebels."

Great sales producers will always have a little baggage and accepting and managing that can bring great rewards. Again, I would never advocate hiring toxic people, no matter what kind of sales skills they bring to the table, but a little baggage is par for the course with top producers.

After identifying a great potential sales candidate, use an assessment company to help underscore your own findings. Find a company that you can work closely with and learn to trust their findings. If you have developed a nice relationship with an assessment company (and please do not make the decision on what company to partner with based on who is cheapest; bad hires are amongst the most costly mistakes you can make), be very careful about dismissing their findings. Their goal is to ensure that you hire the best fit and, while I have yet to hear of any one company that claims 100% accuracy, they are generally very good at what they do. The last thing you want to hear when you believe you have found a great candidate, is that she did not test well. Be very careful about dismissing that counsel: it would be better to use it as a learning process for your ongoing interviewing skill than to pay the steep price for a bad hire.

The last point I want to make is that turnover is not something that anyone feels good about. There are the obvious costs that come with turnover, such as compensation and training, etc. Then there are the less obvious costs such as damaged relationships, both internally and externally. Salespeople who are not very good at sales can still be popular team members and releasing them can sometimes have a short-term negative impact on morale.

Having said that, if you accept that your first responsibility is to construct a sales team that gives your business every opportunity to be successful, a sales team with the fundamental wiring to make sales, build relationships and deliver great experiences for your customers, then you need to stop trying to train horses to climb trees. Turnover becomes an essential element in building your business because the cost of maintaining a mediocre or under-performing team is infinitely more expensive than the alternative. The quicker you accept that no amount of training or coaching, no compensation or incentive plans, no motivational seminars or self-help books will help turn horses into squirrels, the better your business will be for you, your employees and, most of all, for your customers.

Bibliography

First Impressions—Making Up Your Mind After 100-Ms Exposure to a Face, Janine Willis and Alexander Todorov, Princeton University (Copyright 2006 Association for Psychological Science).

State of the Global Workplace, Employee Engagement Insights for Business Leaders Worldwide, Gallup 2011–2012

First, Break All The Rules, Marcus Buckingham and Curt Coffman, Simon & Schuster, 1999

How To Hire And Develop Your Next Top Performer, Greenberg, Sweeney, McGraw-Hill, 2013

Strengths Based Selling, Rutigliano, Brim, Gallup Press, 2011

Never Hire A Bad Salesperson Again, Croner and Abraham, The Richard Abraham Company LLC 2006

The Ultimate Sales Machine, Chet Holmes, Portfolio, 2007

You Can't Send a Duck to Eagle School, Mac Anderson, Simple Truths, 2007

Conversion, The Last Great Retail Metric, Mark Ryski, Author House 2011

What Every Body Is Saying, Joe Navarro with Marvin Karlins, Collins 2008

The Art of Thinking Clearly, Rob Dobelli, Sceptre, 2013

The Perfect Hire, Katherin Graham-Leviss, Entrepreneur Press, 2011

How To Hire A-Players, Eric Herrenkohl, John Wiley & Sons, 2010

Tell To Win, Peter Guber, Crown Business 2007

The Rare Find, Spotting Exceptional Talent Before Everyone Else, George Anders, Portfolio / Penguin 2011

The Art of the Sale, Philip Delves Broughton, The Penguin Press, 2012

There Is An I In Team, Mark De Rond, Harvard Business Review Press, 2012

Winning With People, John Maxwell, Nelson Business, 2004

Selling Retail, John Kawhon with Catherine D. Lawhon, J. Franklin Publisher, Tulsa, Oklahoma 1986

Thriving In The Shadow Of Giants, Eddie Kay, The Armarium Press, 2002

The Retail Doctor, Bob Phibbs, John Wiley & Sons, 2010

Can They Sell, Steve Suggs, Vision Run Publishing, 2012

You Can Read Anyone, David Lieberman, MJF Books, New York 2007

Joyland, Stephen King, A Hard Case Crime Book, 2013

Now, Discover Your Strengths, Marcus Buckingham, Donald Clifton, The Free Press 2001

Top Brain, Bottom Brain, Stephen M. Kosslyn, G. Wayne Miller, Simon & Schuster 2013

Emotional Intelligence, Daniel Goleman, Bantam Books 1995

Animals Inc., Kenneth Tucker, Vandana Allman, Warner Business Company, 2004

Confidence, Rosabeth Moss Kanter, Three Rivers Press, 2004

Trading Up, The New American Luxury, Silverstein & Fiske, Portfolio 2003

Francona, The Red Sox Years, Terry Francona, Dan Shaughnessy, Houghton Mifflin Harcourt 2013

Impulse, Why We Do What We Do Without Knowing It, David Lewis, The Belknap Press of Harvard University Press 2013

Talent Flow, Robert Levin, Joseph Rosse, Jossey-Bass, 2001

Personality Psychology, Domains of Knowledge About Human Nature (Fourth Edition), Randy Larsen, David Buss, McGraw Hill 2010

Ted Williams, A Baseball Life, Michael Seidel, Contemporary Books, Chicago 1991

Learned Optimism, Martin Seligman, Alfred A. Knopf 1991

Confessions of an Advertising Man, David Ogilvy, Southbank Publishing 2011

First Impressions, What You Don't Know About How Others See You, Ann Demarais, Valerie White, Bantam Books 2004

Clutch, While Some People Excel Under Pressure And Others Don't, Paul Sullivan, Portfolio 2010

The Four Minute Mile, Roger Bannister, Dodd, Mead & Company, New York 1955

The Everything Store, Brad Stone, Little, Brown & Company 2013

Made in the USA
Middletown, DE
30 August 2023

37579608R00110